T0209744

FORGOTTEN WARRIORS II

AMPHIBIOUS MARCH ACROSS THE PACIFIC DURING WWII

SECOND EDITION

D. RALPH YOUNG

authorHOUSE®

AuthorHouse™
1663 Liberty Drive
Bloomington, IN 47403
www.authorhouse.com
Phone: 1 (800) 839-8640

© 2020 D. Ralph Young. All rights reserved.

No part of this book may be reproduced, stored in a retrieval system, or
transmitted by any means without the written permission of the author.

Published by AuthorHouse 02/19/2020

ISBN: 978-1-7283-2591-0 (sc)
ISBN: 978-1-7283-2590-3 (hc)
ISBN: 978-1-7283-2589-7 (e)

Library of Congress Control Number: 2019913353

Print information available on the last page.

Any people depicted in stock imagery provided by Getty Images are models,
and such images are being used for illustrative purposes only.
Certain stock imagery © Getty Images.

This book is printed on acid-free paper.

Because of the dynamic nature of the Internet, any web addresses or links contained in
this book may have changed since publication and may no longer be valid. The views
expressed in this work are solely those of the author and do not necessarily reflect the views
of the publisher, and the publisher hereby disclaims any responsibility for them.

CONTENTS

PICTURES

MAPS

TABLE

POEMS

ACKNOWLEDGMENTS

When I wrote this book at ninety years of age, I said then that it was not easy. Now at ninety-four, I refuse to give up and have accepted the challenge of trying to improve my book, *Forgotten Warriors*. I want the reader to be better informed and more knowledgeable about WWII in the Pacific. Also, I want to remove some parts that were meaningful to me in the beginning but now, once documented, can be removed. Above all, I want the world to know that there was a war in the Pacific as well as the Atlantic. There was a Peleliu, Tarawa, Tinian, etc. as well as a Normandy. My hope is that future generations will not forget what my comrades went through by fighting from Aleutian/Guadalcanal to Okinawa in the Pacific Theater during WWII (December 7, 1941–August 15, 1945).

In addition, I want to express my gratitude to Beyond Band of Brothers Tour Group for allowing my wife and me to the get the thrill of a lifetime by taking us back to Guam, Saipan, Tinian, and Okinawa. During this trip, in December 2017, we met many native people (the Chamorros) who have lived on the Marianna Islands for many years and were freed from Japanese slavery in June and July 1944. I find it hard to describe the warmth, kindness, and appreciation they showed for being set free from their Japanese slavery.

I want to acknowledge with great sadness that my shipmate Timothy D. Churchill is no longer with us. Tim composed all the patriotic poetry about our many battles while serving on the USS J. Franklin Bell. Tim passed away on February 16,

2019. Helga, his wife, has agreed to keep his poetry in my book. Tim served his country during three wars (WWII, Korea, and Vietnam) in both the army and the navy. It was during a tour in Germany that he met his beautiful wife Helga. Together, they hosted a ship's reunion in Colorado and were faithful in attending nearly every reunion. Tim retired from the army in 1973. He was buried on February 25, 2019, at the National Cemetery in Sarasota, Florida. He was a great shipmate, and it was an honor to have served with him aboard the USS J. Franklin Bell. Veteran groups around the country will sorely miss his wiliness and ability to create patriotic poetry for their special events.

I continue to thank my wife Janice Louise Young for her support, editing, and encouragement to finish the original and this second edition of my book. All my family members have been great in supporting my work, but my grandson Chad Young has gone the extra mile by designing both the original and second edition covers for my book.

SUMMARY

This is the story of the amphibious march across the Pacific from the Aleutians and Guadalcanal to Okinawa. It tells the experiences of shipmates aboard the USS J. Franklin Bell, which includes the surprise attack on Pearl Harbor and the following battles: the Aleutian Campaign; the Solomon Islands/New Guinea Campaign; and the naval battles of the Java Sea, Coral Sea, Midway, Philippine Sea, and Leyte Gulf. The book also describes the amphibious invasions of the Islands Tarawa, Kwajalein, Eniwetok, Saipan, Tinian, Guam, Leyte, Luzon, Peleliu, Iwo Jima, and finally, Okinawa.

Included is a description of the leadership of the four major commanders of the Pacific Campaign: MacArthur, Nimitz, Spruance, and Halsey.

A history of the USS J. Franklin Bell, her stories of adventure, the author's personal experiences while serving aboard the Bell, and her termination of service are also included.

This edition also includes the names of all Medals of Honor awarded in the Pacific, and several of the citations that illustrate what these men typically did to be selected for the highest award for bravery given by the US government All citations can be found at _www.themedalofhonor.org_. After each battle description, there is a listing of those killed and wounded in that battle.

Finally, included are the contributions made by the coast guard, submarine service, and seabees as well as the women of the US toward victory over the Japanese in World War II.

Last is a list of the original shipmates who boarded the USS J. Franklin Bell on April 2, 1942.

Added to this second edition are the elimination of Admiral Isoroku Yamamoto, the stories of some great heroes during WWII, greater details about the naval battle of Leyte Gulf, mention of the Chamorros of the Marianna Islands, greater detail of the Solomon Islands/New Guinea Campaign, and the story of the sinking of the cruiser USS Indianapolis, just after bringing a vital part for the A-bomb to the island of Tinian.

ABOUT THE AUTHOR

D. Ralph Young grew up on a small farm in central Kentucky during the Great Depression of the early 1930s. He was the youngest of Jake and Bettie Young's eleven children. When his mother suffered a stroke in 1935, his father assigned him to be the house boy. His early childhood was spent following his mother's instructions in cooking, cleaning, washing, ironing, and all other household chores.

At seventeen, he convinced his parents that he should be allowed to enlist in the navy. The reason given was that if he waited to be drafted at eighteen, he would have no choice where he served in the military. His military career took him to the Pacific Theatre of War, where for nearly three years, he served as a gunner's mate on the USS J. Franklin Bell, an amphibious personnel attack ship (APA-16). During his time on the Bell, he survived four major battles in the Pacific (Saipan, Tinian, Leyte, and Okinawa.)

After the war, he married Charlotte Chadwell and raised three children: Dane, Marsha, and David. Charlotte passed away in 2006 after nearly sixty years of marriage. Janice Chappell, Charlotte's first cousin, had just lost her husband some five months earlier when they reconnected. Janice had taught in the embassy school in Jakarta in 1972 when Ralph was doing a power project in Central Java. Since there were no schools for daughter Marsha in central Java, Janice invited her to live with her and attend the embassy school. After this encounter, he never saw Janice again for forty years. They have now been married for more than twelve years and are enjoying life to the fullest. He gives her the credit for his ability to publish four books. Janice's skills in computer software, English language, editing, and overall encouragement have been of tremendous value and made writing these books possible.

Ralph received recognition for his engineering talents by many foreign countries where he practiced his profession as an electric power engineer. These included projects in Saudi Araba, Omen, Iran, Malaysia, Indonesia, and his favorite country, Thailand. In 2006, he was inducted into the University of Kentucky College of Engineering Hall of Distinction.

In December 2017, on a trip back to Saipan and Tinian to visit the beaches where he and some of his shipmates joined the invasion force that landed on D-day, he was awarded a medal by the local natives (the Chamorros) of Saipan and Tinian for Valor in the Pacific during WWII. The medal is inscribed with the wording, "Our Grateful Islands Remember."

SEVERAL REASONS FOR WRITING THIS BOOK

The deafening sound of battle was everywhere on the island of Peleliu when the marine commander said, "We have a wounded comrade on the front line of battle, and I need a stretcher detail of four men to go to the front and bring him back here."

Among the four volunteers was Richard Kraus, an eighteen-year-old Marine from Minneapolis, Minnesota, who was experiencing his first battle on the island of Peleliu in 1944. As the four men advanced toward the front lines, the machine gun fire and hand grenades launching became so intense that they had to take cover in a foxhole. Suddenly, two men were seen approaching their foxhole, and a password was demanded. Instead of a password, the four mariners received a hand grenade tossed into the group. Richard Kraus threw his body onto the grenade, absorbing the full impact of the explosion and thereby saving the lives of the other three comrades. For this, he was awarded the Medal of Honor.

Other than his family, how many people would remember Richard Kraus? Even fewer would remember that there was a battle on the island of Peleliu. Therefore, I feel compelled to write about the war in the Pacific and all those battles and soldiers that have been forgotten.

It seems that we celebrate Normandy every year but not Peleliu, where during the invasion, we had twice the number of American casualties as the D-day invasion of Normandy. I could probably count on one hand all those who have not heard about Normandy. This book is in no way intended to degrade all or any of the many sacrifices made by our troops at Normandy. They deserve all the attention and respect they have received. However, the forces at Peleliu and other forgotten battles in the Pacific call for comparable notice as well.

The troops who fought in the Pacific are veterans who have been mostly forgotten by the present generation. Others feel the same as I do. For example, an article in *Naval History* titled "Peleliu: The Forgotten Battle" by Maj. Henry Donigan, who fought there and lived to write and publish the story in September 1994, states,

> Fifty years ago, in a forgotten backwater of the Central Pacific, Marines, soldiers and sailors fought the Japanese in one of the most savage and costly battles in World War II. The assault on the island of Peleliu compares to the most famous battles in American history in terms of ferocity and valor. Yet this battle has been all-but-forgotten except by a few historians and the valiant men who fought there.

All these soldiers of World War II were from a generation called the greatest generation by author Tom Brokaw in his book by the same name. They were people from all walks of life who trusted our government and loved our country. They had a love so deep that they were willing to die for our country's freedoms. They never asked for anything from our government other than, "Where and when do you want me to start defending my country?"

I am honored to have throughout my book poetry written by my shipmate on the USS J. Franklin Bell, Timothy Churchill. In his patriotic poem, "A Celebration of Our Forces," he so eloquently wrote,

A Celebration of Our Forces

You heard your country's call to arms,
Once more to take a stand,
Your brave response was loud and clear,
"Keep freedom in your land."

You marched away with fearless stride,
You fought on foreign soil;
With courage, calm, and sacrifice,
You challenged war's turmoil.

You came from every walk of life,
To heed our nation's call;
You're American's Forces, Guard, Reserve
You are our heroes all.
Your stand is to defend the right,
You are our country's pride;
You bravely march into harm's way,
Your cause is justified.

So, march today, you honored vets,
With banner, standing tall.
May God bless each and every one,
We thank you one and all.

 Patriotic poetry is written by Timothy D. Churchill (1926-2019). This book is in his Honor and Memory.

It all began on December 7, 1941, a day to be remembered. I recall the date vividly and can still hear the announcer on the radio saying the Japanese had attacked Pearl Harbor. My best friend, Bill Scheuer and I were hitchhiking home from attending a movie in Stanford, Kentucky. The driver of the car was listening to the radio and told us that the Japanese had just bombed Pearl Harbor.

I was sixteen years old at the time. Everything pointed toward a long war, and there was little doubt that the military draft would be lowered from twenty-one to eighteen. I just knew I would be off to the war at eighteen years of age.

Initially, I wanted to be a pilot. I can still remember walking to the back fields on our farm to bring the cows up for milking and watching the planes in the sky as they flew over our farm. I could visualize myself at the control of a powerful plane, wearing a leather helmet and a scarf flying in the wind.

In addition, another good friend, Glen Faulkner, had researched aviation and talked about flying all the time. The fact that I did not have enough education to become a pilot was a problem and therefore necessitated a reality check on my part about my future in the war effort.

At that period, one did not get to select a branch of service if he waited to be drafted. The government put draftees where they were most needed. So, with all this in mind, when I became seventeen, I convinced my parents that I should enlist in the navy because I would then be allowed to finish high school before having to report for training.

Therefore, I enlisted when I was seventeen, but I did not have to report for duty until I was eighteen, after high school graduation. My boot camp training was at Great Lakes, Illinois. But this book is not meant to be about me. (A book about me is titled *The Power of a Mother's Prayer.*) This book is about all those sailors, soldiers, and marines (including me) who fought in the Pacific and now, in my opinion, have almost been forgotten.

It seems that we celebrate the invasion of Normandy, the Battle of the Bulge, and the European Theater of war every year; but missing from such recognitions are invasions in Peleliu, Tarawa, and Tinian, etc. How many times have you heard V-J Day verses V-E Day? Another example is the World War II Museum in New Orleans, which was founded in the year 2000 and waited until 2015 to begin an exhibit titled "The Road to Tokyo." "The Road to Berlin" has been already completed. Have those in charge forgotten who attacked us at Pearl Harbor? I say this with tongue in cheek, because it is just great to have this museum dedicated to the memory of World War II veterans, and I did make the contribution the New Orleans Museum requested to bring the Pacific Theater of war up to equal status with the European Theater of war. Also, the museum is fast becoming number one for World War II history.

Since there are hundreds of books that analyze World War II very well, this book is meant to summarize some of the major battles in the Pacific and briefly answer the questions of what, where, when, and why. It is not intended to provide an in-depth analysis of every battle across the Pacific during World War II.

Rather, it addresses only those that essentially apply to me and my ship the USS J. Franklin Bell.

What kind of enemy did our Pacific Theater troops face? In Edwin P. Hoyt's book *War in the Pacific*, he describes the Japanese code produced by Hideki Tojo in a pamphlet called "Senjinkum" for the Japanese soldier. The new army held that the emperor was divine, being above men, and that the lives of everyone in the Japanese empire had to be dedicated to imperial service. Don't stay alive in dishonor; don't die in such a way as to leave a bad name behind you. This philosophy lead to allied medical corpsmen being shot while attending the wounded, allied chaplains being shot while administering last rites, and allied soldiers being bayoneted because they were too weak to walk: a medieval enemy with a barbarian philosophy. A Japanese slogan used by the army in the early 1940s said that "To die for the Emperor was to live forever."

I do not mean to imply that all my comrades were saints. In the heat of battle, we did some things that were not very pretty, such as cutting off an ear and attaching to a belt. But these were isolated cases and not standard operating procedures, as they were with the Japanese soldier.

If you want further proof of how vicious the Japanese military was trained to act, read about the rape of Nanking or consider the words of China's Chiang Kai-Shek about the 250,000 Chinese executed because of the Doolittle raid on Japan. This inhumane act was for allowing the B-25 bombers to land at Chinese airports after a surprise bombing of Japan. On the other hand, the German and Italian soldiers were tough fighters, but they were human beings, not barbarians.

Another example of the breed of enemy we fought in the Pacific is in the survival rate for the prisoners of war (POWs). For those captured by the Germans and Italians, the death rate was a little more than 1 percent. For those under Japanese control, the death rate was more than 40 percent. The fanatical attitude of the Japanese soldiers is readily explained by looking at the kill-to-wounded ratio. This ratio was about three wounded for each one killed in the US military during World War II. But for the Japanese, it was the reverse—about eighteen killed for each one wounded—because Japanese soldiers refused to surrender. Compare the above with what Timothy Churchill says about the American veteran.

Patriotic poetry is written by Timothy D. Churchill (1926-2019). This book is in his Honor and Memory.

The American Veteran

America's veterans, young and old
Have made our nation proud;
We salute you for your service now,
And sing your praise aloud

We know the sacrifices you've made,
To serve and face the foe;
And save the freedom for our land,
That all the world should know.

America's veterans, always first,
And always in our prayers;
As you march to war, in any war,
America always cares.

And just as surely, we can share,
Our patriotic dream,
That peace returns, when you return,
With victory to redeem.

The ones who marched in former time,
Some gone, but honored still,
And those who wave the flag today,
Salute, as veterans will.

And so we take this time to say,
Our "thanks" to one and all;
For those who serve our nation's cause.
Salute, you're standing tall.

Another reason for writing this book is that I am proud to have served on the USS J. Franklin Bell. It did not have the prestige of a battleship or cruiser nor the beautiful lines and swagger of a destroyer. But the APAs (amphibious personnel assault ships) were always in the middle of the action and served our nation well. It should be noted that most of the rungs in the ladder in our climb from Guadalcanal toward the mainland of Japan were not won by battleships', cruisers', and destroyers' bombardments of beaches. This was always a necessary first step in any invasion, but in every invasion, the battle was won by putting soldiers, marines, and naval personnel on the beaches and supplying them with the equipment and supplies needed in battle. The landing area had to be kept clear for incoming troops' supplies and equipment. This is why it was important for each ship to send a beach party to the landing area with the invasion force. It can be said that it was a great joint effort.

My children joke about the many letters I write to newspaper editors on subjects that concern me. The fact is that I have written twice as many as they know about, because after getting my opinion off my chest, I often toss them in the wastebasket. But this time, I will finish the course for all my comrades and shipmates who fought and died in that vast, intimidating, and unimaginable (but sometimes beautiful) Pacific Ocean. In addition, this second edition is also written for those who are still alive. I will be self-publishing, in book form, with my thoughts and prayers in their honor on every page.

When I first started to think about writing this book, I went on the internet to research World War II in the Pacific. It was during this early stage of research that I came upon a picture of a young marine by the name of Richard Kraus from Minneapolis, Minnesota, whom I mentioned in the opening paragraphs. Richard looked youthful, as did the millions of us just like him. The thought that we had to engage in combat with the battle-hardened, China-occupied, vicious, and cruel Japanese soldiers was another inspiration for me to research and write this book.

The real reason for the lack of attention to the war in the Pacific is unknown to me, because records show that the Pacific Theater of war had about 50 percent of the total casualties in WWII. So, if we are going by total sacrifices, the Pacific Theater should have equal attention.

The bias continues to this day (April 2019), as the World War II museum in New Orleans is soliciting funds for a seventy-fifty anniversary celebration of June 6, 1944: D-day at Normandy. To my knowledge, there are no plans for a seventy-fifty anniversary of D-day at Saipan, which occurred nine days later with nearly twice the casualties during the invasion of Saipan as our Americans casualties on D-day at Normandy.

Richard Kraus at eighteen:
the Battle of Peleliu
Courtesy Medal of Honor
Org public domain

D. Ralph Young at
eighteen on board the
USS J. Franklin Bell
Courtesy of D. Ralph Young

Yes, we were very young back in those days, and when I look at a picture of Richard, I get a guilty feeling for being more than ninety-four years of age when Richard had to die so young. Young men like Richard should not have had to die in wars between nations. I just wish that the leaders of all our nations could somehow be exposed for a few days in the front lines of battle and contend with the smell of human flesh decaying right before them—a smell never forgotten regardless of age. This would go a long way toward creating permanent peace in the world.

Other than my own experience and those of a few shipmates, all my information has come from the sources listed in the bibliography found at the end of this book. My target is for a quick reference describing each major battle that will identify casualties, loss of ships and aircraft, and Medals of Honor awarded.

There is one more important reason for writing this book. I am one of the few survivors left to tell the story of this great ship. The USS *J. Franklin Bell* received seven battle stars for her contribution as she moved across the Pacific Theater of war toward Japan during World War II.

These battles were relived over and over by my shipmates for twenty-one years after shipmate Chet Maki made the first one happen in 1987. I was proud to have hosted three such reunions in Kentucky, and I for one wish they had not stopped. But age and travel caught up with most shipmates.

Attendance at tenth reunion in Canton, Ohio
Courtesy of D. Ralph Young—public domain

Attendance at last reunion in 2009 in Tyler, Texas
Courtesy of D. Ralph Young—public domain

The above pictures indicated how our number of shipmates had reduced over an eleven-year period (1987–1998.) Since the last reunion was in 2009, I might just be one of the few remaining survivors.

During the reunions, we fought the battles over and over, and I detected that the intensity of our many battles increased from year to year—or maybe, like our Kentucky bourbon, they just got better with age. The fact is that we were all very young that day in December when the Japanese attacked Pearl Harbor. The following poem, "The Day the Music Died," reflected what Bell shipmate Timothy Churchill had to say about our country and the attack on Pearl Harbor.

The Day the Music Died

The music from the radio,
Died so suddenly;
I caught my breath and dropped a dish,
That day of infamy.

Remembering" Pearl Harbor,"
As a day in time for some;
A day's event to change the world,
And shape what was to come.

Pearl Harbor now a peaceful place,
Where havoc was in store;
That day so many years ago,
When aircraft bombed our shore.

America woke to bombs and fire,
That turned our peaceful tide,
No more would life go on the same,
That day the music died.

For those who still recall that day,
Their minds remember well,
And live again just where they were,
And wept for those who fell.

The history of our nation's plight,
Brings honor, then as now.
Our brave American response,
Kept "victory" as our vow.

Remembering "Pearl Harbor Event,"
As source of pride;
Salute our nation's gallantry,
Our Forces, far and wide.

The courage of our fighting men,
Reflects the honor due,
To all of those who passed before,
And those we never knew.

WHY THERE WAS A WAR IN THE PACIFIC

The country of Japan had a population of nearly one hundred million people and allowed itself to be governed by the military in the late 1930s. There were two factions within the military: one that wanted to expand north and another that wanted to expand south. The north won the internal battle and began an expansion north, but they suffered defeat at every turn where they met the Russians. This brought a pause during which the south supporters convinced the military that an advance toward Malay and Dutch East Indies would be easier if the US Navy could be defeated or neutralized. It should be noted that at this period, the Japanese had enough current reserves of oil and other resources to last about one year. The Malay's tin and rubber and the East Indie's oil made a south adventure very attractive.

Peace between Japanese and the US did not appear possible for two reasons: first, the US had cut off oil shipments to Japan, which infuriated the military. Second, the US demanded a withdrawal from their occupation of China.

At the start of 1940, the Japanese army was about 475,000 men strong. However, there were another nearly eight hundred thousand army reserve troops, and they were tough and well-trained to do whatever was necessary to win the battle. Through their many years of war with China, most Japanese soldiers were battle-hardened.

Another factor influencing Japanese's action is that reserves could be called into action. These standby troops had undergone the same detailed training as the regular army. The youthful Japanese were often given a hero status even before they left home for training by family, friends, and the government. The Japanese soldiers were dedicated to die for the emperor and were trained to win. Losing was not an option.

Also, throughout Asia, there was the feeling of inferiority to white people. Japan was intent on driving the Americans, British, and Dutch from Asia. This, in all probability, had some influence on the Japanese being accepted so readily in Burma, Thailand, Indochina, Indonesia, and other areas of the Pacific. Japanese historians concluded that the year 1940 was the 2,600th anniversary of their nation. As a result, a large celebration was scheduled by the emperor. This resulted in a high wave of enthusiasm for the nation. On January 1, 1941, all the Japanese political leaders vowed to give up their rights and join the cause as set forth by the army leaders. This meant that an adventure in some direction was a foregone conclusion. In fact, Japanese Admiral Isoroku Yamamoto is credited with saying, "The goal of our nation is that all eight corners of the world would be under one roof." To achieve success in Asia, the Japanese knew that they had to neutralize the US Navy. So, the attack on Pearl Harbor was developed. In fact, most of 1941 was used by the Japanese Navy in preparing for the attack. This was done at Kagoshima on the southern tip of Kyushu. They had set up a model of Pearl Harbor for training using specially designed torpedoes because of the shallow water they would experience at Pearl Harbor.

Since many of us were away from the US during most of the war, I have elected to include some facts on life in America during that period. In 1941, Americans in the US were busy following the war in Europe, which was dominating world affairs. Attention was given to events like the completion of Mount Rushmore featuring US presidents by Gutzon Borglum and the development of the United Service Organization (USO), which provided coffee, donuts, and entertainment to US military personnel who were being drafted at the age of twenty-one. During this period in the US, a new home could be bought for the average price of $4,075, the cost of a gallon of gas was $0.12, a new car was $850, and a house could be rented for $32 per month. President Roosevelt signed the Land Lease Act providing military aid to the Allies, the Willys Jeep was introduced for use by the US Army, Glen Miller brought us the "Chattanooga Choo Choo," and the Andrews Sisters sang, "I'll Be with You in Apple Blossom Time."

In charge of the Japanese attack on Pearl Harbor was Admiral Yamamoto. His plan was to inflict enough damage to the US fleet so that it would not be able to interfere with their invasion of all southeast Asia. Yamamoto was willing to commit six aircraft carriers to the surprise attack, which did not go well with the battleship commanders, because they considered this too much of a risk and exposure of their naval aircraft and resources. But Yamamoto felt that risk was necessary in a time of war.

On November 10, 1941, the Japanese began their journey to an island in the Kuriles where they assembled to stock up on oil and supplies previously stashed for this purpose. Then on December 2, 1941, they departed for the surprise attack on Pearl Harbor. At the same time, two Japanese Ambassadors were meeting with Secretary of State Hull in Washington, DC, talking peace.

THE ATTACK ON PEARL HARBOR

The mindless rejoicing at home is really appalling; it makes me fear that the first blow against Tokyo will make them wilt at once ... I only wish that (the Americans) had also had three carriers at Hawaii.

—Admiral Isoroku Yamamoto, Commander in Chief of the Japanese Navy

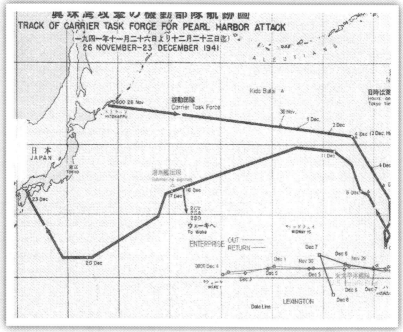

The routes taken by the Japanese fleet for their attack on Pearl Harbor and return to Japan (Courtesy of Wikimedia public domain)

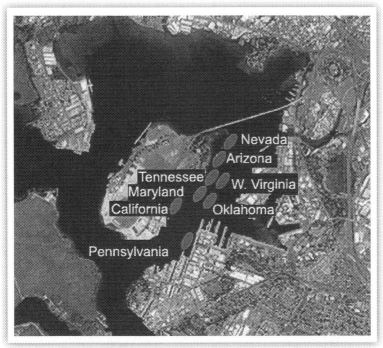

Pearl Harbor on December 7, 1941
(Courtesy of Naval Archive public domain)

The surprise attack on Pearl Harbor occurred at 7:48 a.m. Hawaiian time on December 7, 1941 (12:48 p.m. Eastern.) There were similar (but not simultaneous, due to time zone differences) attacks on the Philippines, Malaya, Singapore, and Hong Kong, which brought the Netherlands and England into the war along with the US. The attack came as a shock to the American people, and the US declared war on Japan the following day, December 8, 1941. Germany and Italy declared war on the US on December 11, 1941, and the US responded with a war declaration on them the same day.

The Japanese chose a weekend for the attack because they had noted that the US battleship commanders had always tried to get their crews in port for weekend shore leave. They also considered this a weakness in the Americans and felt their soldiers were far superior. In addition, at that time, the most prestigious ship in any navy was the battleship, which made them the number one target.

The Japanese had hoped that our aircraft carriers would be in port. But they were out at sea, and they did not know where they were. This, in all probability, caused them to cut short the complete destruction of Pearl Harbor, because they left the area without doing any damage to the navy yard, the above ground oil tank farms, or the submarine base. Another thought by many is that the Japanese underestimated the will and determination of the American people and expected a short war with the US.

Photograph taken by Japanese pilot of Battleship Row. The smoke in the background is from the hanger and planes at Hickman Field. (Courtesy-National Archives-Public Domain)

To be in Pearl Harbor that day had to be a frightening experience for those who awakened to the sound of bombs exploding. In addition, the General Quarters alarm was being piped down, and loud gunfire was in the immediate area. This required many of the crew to dress on their way to their General Quarters station. The defenders were totally unprepared, with ammunition lockers locked and aircraft parked close together for the purpose of protecting from sabotage. A total of 323 Japanese planes made up the two waves. The first waves of 152 planes were led by torpedo bombers, with their target being the battleships. Then the dive bombers came with their attack on the air bases across Oahu. The second wave of 171 planes concentrated their attack on Bellows Field and Ford Island.

Ninety minutes after it began, the attack was over. The death and wounded totals are listed below. Nearly half of the US fatalities were caused by the forward magazine explosion of the battleship *Arizona*.

US sailors trying to control the fires (Courtesy of National Archives public domain)

I have never been overly impressed with the memorial for that ship—maybe because it did not say anything to me and looked like an odd structure. My research tells me that the designer, Alfred Preis, meant to convey a sagging center with the ends being strong and vigorous, meaning initial defeat and ultimate victory. Perhaps it will look different to me the next time I visit.

The Japanese planners decided to select a location where their troubled planes, unable to return to their carriers, could land for rescue. They chose the island of Niihau. A zero flown by Petty Officer Shigenori Nishikaichi was damaged during the attack on Wheeler Air Force Base and again on landing. The officer was helped from the wreckage by a native Hawaiian who was aware of tensions between the US and Japanese. He took the pilot's maps and other documents. The local inhabitants had no telephone or radio contacts, so they were completely unaware of the attack by the Japanese earlier in the day. The Japanese officer enlisted the support of three Japanese American residents to recover his documents. During the struggle that followed, the Japanese officer was killed, and a civilian was wounded. One of the Japanese Americans committed suicide, and his wife and the other were sent to prison. It sounds awful when you think about our putting 110,000 Japanese Americans in internment camps. But the above incident probably played a key role in that decision.

The war with Japan created some bizarre events, such as a two-day battle against no one. It was reported by the *Los Angeles Times* that on February 24 and 25, 1942, unexplained lights in the sky were thought to be Japanese planes, but they were caused by lost weather balloons and mistaken as enemy aircraft. The result was the sky being pummeled for two nights with round after round of ammunition. Each base involved thought the other was being attacked by Japanese bombers. Shortly afterward, Secretary of the Navy Frank Knox admitted it was a false alarm.

During World War II, there were 464 recipients of the Medal of Honor, with 266 being awarded posthumously. This book includes the names of those awarded the Medal of Honor throughout the Pacific Campaign. In addition, several descriptions are included so the reader can understand what it takes to be awarded the Medal of Honor. For an in-depth description on any Medal of Honor awarded, go to the website _www.themedalofhonor.org_, where the award can be read or printed. There were 197 awardees in the Pacific Theater. The criteria for being awarded the Medal of Honor is for conspicuous gallantry and intrepidity at the risk of life, above and beyond the call of duty. The medal is authorized by Congress and awarded by the president. A total of fifteen were awarded for the attack on Pearl Harbor. A short description for each is included.

Each Medal of Honor awardee is a story of commitment and sacrifice above and beyond the call of duty. Many instances are recorded of individuals giving their lives to save their comrades. As you read each one, pause for a moment, and contemplate what these men have done to preserve the freedoms and the beautiful way of life we now enjoy here in the United States of America during the twenty-first century.

THE MARCH ACROSS THE PACIFIC TOWARD JAPAN

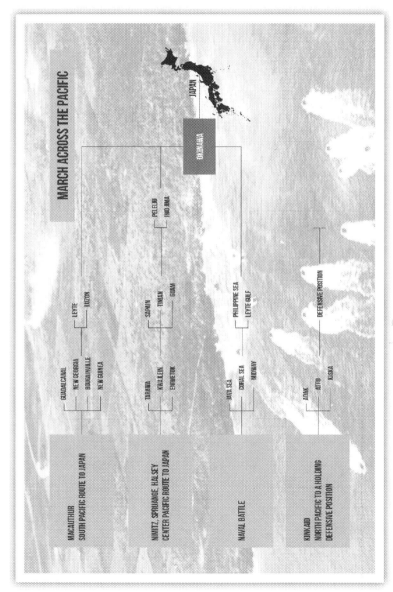

The flow and sequence of the battles across the Pacific (Courtesy of Chadwell Young)

Table 1: Troop, ship, and aircraft casualties at Pearl Harbor

	USA	JAPAN
Killed	2403*	64
Wounded	1178*	-
Captured	-	1

*USA Civilian Casualties: an additional 68 killed and 35 wounded

	USA		JAPAN	
	Destroyed	Damaged	Destroyed	Damaged
Battleships	4	-	-	-
Cruisers	3	-	-	-
Destroyers	3	-	-	-
Other-types	5	4	-	-
Midget-Subs	-	-	4	1
Aircraft	188	158	29	-

Below are listed the fifteen Medals of Honor awarded for the Pearl Harbor attack. I have included a short description of each because they need to be recognized. Detailed descriptions can be seen at _www.themedalofhonor.org_.

Marvyn Bennion, Captain, US Navy, born May 5, 1887, in Vemon, Utah. Captain Bennion was the commanding officer of the USS West Virginia with extraordinary courage beyond the call of duty during the attack on Pearl Harbor on December 7, 1941. After being mortally wounded while fighting to save his ship, he strongly protested while being carried from his bridge by Dorie Miller and other crew members. Using one arm to hold his wound closed, he bled to death while still commanding his crew. For this action, he was awarded the Medal of Honor.

John William Finn, Lieutenant, US Navy, born July 15, 1909, in Los Angeles, California. Although painfully wounded many times, he continued to man his 50-caliber machine gun and to return enemy fire vigorously with telling effect and complete disregard for his own personal safety. Although painfully wounded many times, he continued to man his gun and return the enemy fire. It was only by specific orders that he was persuaded to leave his post to seek medical treatment. He returned to the squadron area and actively supervised the rearming of returning planes.

Frances C. Flaherty, Ensign, US Navy Reserve, born March 15, 1919, in Charlotte, Michigan. When the USS Oklahoma was about to capsize and orders were given to abandon ship, he remained in a turret holding a flashlight so the remainder of the turret crew could escape, thereby sacrificing his own life.

Samuel Glenn Fuqua, Captain, US Navy, born October 15, 1899, in Laddonia, Missouri. Despite being knocked unconscious by an enemy bomb, he recovered to lead in fighting a fire that was spreading throughout the ship. His amazingly calm and cool manner and excellent judgment inspired all those who saw him and resulted in the saving of many lives.

Edwin Joseph Hill, Chief Boatswain, born October 4, 1894, in Philadelphia, Pennsylvania. During the strafing and bombing at Pearl Harbor, he led his men of the line handling to the quays. He cast off the lines and swam back to the ship. While attempting to release the anchors, he was killed by the explosion of several bombs.

Herbert Charpoit Jones, Ensign, US Navy Reserve, born December 1, 1918, in Los Angeles, California. Ens. Jones organized and led a party to supply ammunition to the antiaircraft battery on the USS California after the mechanical hoist was put out of action. He was fatally wounded, and when two men attempted to take him away, he refused to leave, saying, "Leave me alone! I am done for. Get out before the magazines go off."

Isaac Campbell Kidd, Rear Admiral, US Navy, born March 26, 1884, in Cleveland, Ohio. Rear Admiral Kidd immediately went to the bridge as Commander Battleship Division One, where he courageously discharged his duties as Senior Officer Afloat until the USS Arizona, his flagship, blew up from a magazine explosion and a direct bomb hit on the bridge, resulting in his death.

Jackson Charles Pharris, Lieutenant, US Navy, born June 26, 1912, in Columbus, Georgia. Lieutenant Pharris was stunned and severely injured by the concussion of the first torpedo. He recovered quickly and acted on his own to set up a hand-to-hand supply for the antiaircraft guns. Twice rendered unconscious by the nauseating fumes, he persisted in his desperate effort to speed up the supply of ammunition. He risked his life several times to enter flooding compartments to drag unconscious shipmates to safety. He was largely responsible for keeping the California in action during the attack.

Thomas James Reeves, Radio Electrician (Warrant Officer), US Navy, born December 9, 1895, in Thomaston, Connecticut. After the mechanized hoists were put out of action on the USS California, on his own initiative in a burning passageway, Reeves assisted in the maintenance of ammunition supply by hand to the antiaircraft guns until he was overcome by smoke and fire, which resulted in his death.

Donald Kirby Ross, Machinist Mate, US Navy, born December 8, 1910, in Beverly, Kansas. Machinist Mate Ross forced his men to leave the forward dynamo room due to smoke, steam, and heat. He continued doing all his duties until he became unconscious and was rescued and resuscitated. Ross returned to secure the forward dynamo room and then proceeded to the aft dynamo room, where he was again rendered unconscious by exhaustion. Again, recovering consciousness, he returned to his station on the USS Nevada.

Robert R. Scott, Machinist Mate First Class, US Navy, born July 13, 1915, in Massillon, Ohio. The air compressor compartment in the USS California, to which Scott was assigned as his battle station, was flooded as a result of a torpedo hit. The remainder of the personnel evacuated that compartment, but Scott refused to leave, saying, "This is my station, and I will stay and give air as long as the guns are going."

Peter Tomich, Chief Watertender, US Navy, born June 3, 1893, in Prolog, Austria. Although realizing that the ship was capsizing as a result of enemy bombing and torpedoing, Tomich remained at his post in the engineering plant of the USS Utah until he saw that all boilers were secure and all fire room personnel had left their stations, and by doing so, he lost his life.

Franklin Van Valkenburgh, Captain, US Navy, born April 5, 1888, in Minneapolis, Minnesota. As commanding officer of the USS Arizona, he gallantly fought from his ship until the ammunition magazine exploded and a direct bomb hit to the bridge, which resulted in his death.

James Richard Ward, Seaman First Class, US Navy, born September 10, 1921, in Springfield, Ohio. When it was seen that the USS Oklahoma was going to capsize and the order was given to abandon ship, Ward remained in a turret holding a flashlight so the remainder of the turret crew could see to escape, thereby sacrificing his own life.

Cassin Young, Commander, US Navy, born March 6, 1894, in Washington, District of Columbia. Comdr. Young's ship, the USS Vestal, was moored alongside the Arizona. When the ammunition magazine exploded, it blew him off the ship. He managed to swim back to his ship through oil and fire to take command of his ship and move away from the Arizona. He eventually beached his ship to keep it from sinking.

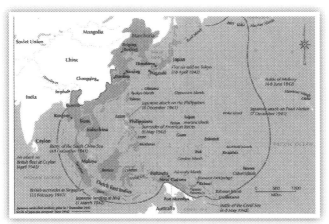

**The shaded dark area indicates the part of Asia
controlled by the Japanese in early 1942
(Courtesy of Jacqueline Goins Bartek)**

After Pearl Harbor, the Japanese quickly gained control over a huge area of the Pacific from the Philippines to Burma to the Aleutians to the Solomons' (see above map). It appeared that the Japanese misjudged the will and determination of the American people and as a result overextended themselves by occupying such a large area that with any substantial losses, they did not have the resources to respond. This became evident during the naval battles of the Cora Sea and Midway, with the advances of the Japanese checked at the Cora Sea. A month later, with the US going on the offensive at Midway (a miraculous Midway), they never again stopped being the aggressor until victory was completed.

WORLD WAR II LEADERSHIP IN THE PACIFIC THEATER

A military man can scarcely pride himself on having smitten a sleeping enemy; it is more a matter of shame, simply for the one smitten.

—Admiral Isoroku Yamamoto, Commander in Chief of the Japanese Navy (about Pearl Harbor, 1942)

When this war is over, the Japanese language will be spoken only in hell.

—Admiral Bill Halsey (December 7, 1941)

ADMIRAL CHESTER M. NIMITZ

Chester W. Nimitz, fleet admiral of the United States Navy, was born on February 24, 1885, and died on February 20, 1966. He played a major role in the naval history of World War II as Commander in Chief of the United States Pacific Fleet. He was the leading US Navy authority on submarines and was a key factor in building the first nuclear-powered submarine, the USS Nautilus.

His father had died six months prior to his birth, and he was heavily influenced by his grandfather, who had been a past German Merchant Marine. The lesson learned from his grandfather was that the sea, like life itself, is a stern taskmaster. The best way to get along with either is to learn all you can and then do your best and not worry—especially about things over which you have no control.

Originally, Adm. Nimitz applied for West Point, but no appointments were available. He was told by Congressman James L. Slayden that he had one appointment available for the navy and that he would award it to the best candidate available. Nimitz thought that this was his only opportunity for advanced education and really applied himself to win the award. He graduated from the Naval Academy seventy in a class of 114 on January 30, 1905.

In early 1942, the US Joint Chief of Staff divided the Pacific theater of war into three regions: the southwest Pacific under General MacArthur, the Pacific Ocean areas and the southeast

Pacific, which were under Adm. Chester W. Nimitz, who was responsible for all land, air, and sea operations in his areas. The third area was the Aleutian Islands, where we only established a defensive position.

On September 2, 1945, Adm. Nimitz signed for the United States when the Japanese formally surrendered on board the USS Missouri in Tokyo Bay. Admiral Nimitz suffered a stroke in late 1965 and died on February 20, 1966. He was buried with full military honors at the Golden Gate National Cemetery in San Bruno, California, where he lies alongside his wife and longtime friends Admiral Raymond A. Spruance, Admiral Richmond K. Turner, and Admiral Charles A. Lockwood. Burial arrangements were made by all of them while they were yet living.

GENERAL DOUGLAS MACARTHUR

Douglas MacArthur was born on January 26, 1880 and died on April 5, 1964. Raised in a military family in the old West, he attended the United States Military Academy at West Point, where he graduated first in his class of 1903. His tour of duty included Superintendent of West Point after his assignment in Europe, where he was promoted to Brigadier General. In World War I, he was nominated for the Medal of Honor and was awarded the Distinguished Service Cross twice and the Silver Star seven times.

General MacArthur retired from the military in 1937 and became military advisor for the Philippine government. He was recalled to active duty in 1941 and given command of the army forces in the Far East.

On the night of March 12, 1942, MacArthur and a select group were ordered by President Roosevelt to relocate to Australia. He and his family were taken to Mindanao by PT boat, where they boarded a B-17 and were flown to Australia. It was at this time that he made the speech, "I came through, and I shall return." When asked by Washington to change the "I" to a "we," he ignored the request, which was typical of MacArthur.

In July 1944, President Roosevelt summoned both MacArthur and Nimitz to meet him in Hawaii "to determine the phase of action against the Japanese." Nimitz made the case for attacking Formosa, but MacArthur convinced Roosevelt that there was an obligation to liberate the Philippines. Therefore, the road to Japan was going to be through the Philippines with the attack on the beaches of Leyte on October 20, 1944.

On August 29, 1945, MacArthur was placed in charge of the rebuilding of the Japanese government. By 1946, he had developed a new Japanese constitution that instituted a parliamentary system of government under which the emperor acted only on the advice of his ministers.

ADMIRAL RAYMOND SPRUANCE

Raymond Spruance was born in Baltimore, Maryland on July 3, 1886. He died on December 13, 1969. During that period, he attended Indianapolis public schools and graduated from Shortridge High School. He followed that by graduating from the Naval Academy in 1906. While his first duty assignment was on the battleship USS Iowa, he also served on the battleship USS Minnesota and was commander on five different destroyers before 1916, when he was transferred to the battleship USS Pennsylvania for her commissioning until 1917. He followed this service with several years of being associated with the Naval War College.

At the beginning of World War II, Adm. Spruance commanded four heavy cruisers and support ships, which were attached to a task force built around the aircraft carrier USS Enterprise, commanded by Vice Admiral William F. Halsey Jr. Admiral Spruance's claim to fame came by a stroke of luck. He was nearby when Admiral Halsey was stricken with a bad case of shingles and was hospitalized just before the battle of the Midway. Halsey recommended Spruance to Nimitz and suggested to Spruance that he lean heavily on his battle-proven expert in carrier warfare, Captain Miles Browning.

The resulting battle saw the sinking of all four of the Japanese fleet carriers with one US carrier being lost. The additional loss of aircraft and pilots by the Japanese during this battle nearly depleted their ability to fight in the air. Thus, was born the kamikaze as a Japanese offensive weapon.

Admiral Spruance's coolness and patience at just the right moment caused historian Samuel E. Morison to write, "Fletcher did well but Spruance was superb: Calm, Collected, and Decisive. Yet receptive to advice, keeping in his mind the picture of widely disparate forces, yet boldly seizing every opening, Raymond A. Spruance emerged from the battle as one of the greatest admirals in American Naval history."

To many people, Admiral Spruance was a mystery, because he never expressed his feelings, prejudices, hopes, or fears. He was very active and thought nothing of walking several miles a day. He once said, "Some people think that when I am quiet that I am in deep important thought, but the truth is that my mind is a complete blank." He loved wearing old khakis and work shoes and spending time in his greenhouse and garden.

Admiral Spruance died in Pebble Beach, California on December 13, 1969. He was buried alongside his wife, Fleet Admiral Chester Nimitz, Admiral Richmond K. Turner, and Admiral Charles A. Lockwood, an arrangement made by all of them while living.

ADMIRAL WILLIAM HALSEY JR.

William Halsey Jr. was born on October 30, 1882, in Elizabeth, New Jersey, and died on August 16, 1959, while holidaying on Fishers Island, New York. Early in life, and after waiting two years for an appointment to the United States Naval Academy, Halsey decided to study medicine at the University of Virginia. After his first year, he received the appointment to the Naval Academy and interred in the fall of 1900. Initially, he served on the battleship Missouri. But torpedoes and torpedo boats became his specialties.

In 1934, Admiral Ernest King offered Halsey the command of the aircraft carrier USS Saratoga contingent upon him completing a course of an air observer. Captain Halsey elected to enroll as a cadet for the full twelve-week naval aviator course, which caused his wife to say to their daughter, "What do you think that the old fool is doing now? He is learning to fly!" So, on May 15, 1935, at the age of fifty-two, he got his wings. He was the oldest man in naval history to accomplish this feat.

Since navy intelligence thought that the war with Japanese would start with a surprise attack on Wake Island, Admiral Halsey was ordered to take the USS Enterprise to ferry aircraft to Wake to reinforce the marines. Halsey had given orders to sink any ship sighted and shoot down any aircraft sighted. When protests occurred about this decision, Halsey said, "We will shoot first and argue afterwards." The Enterprise was delayed in its return to Pearl Harbor on December 6, 1941, by a storm. The ship was still two hundred miles out to sea when word of the Pearl Harbor attack was received. Admiral Halsey and the USS Enterprise searched to the south and west for the Japanese fleet, but it had departed to the north and west.

In early 1942, Admiral Halsey was overcome with a chronic skin condition that was so serious that he was sent by cruiser to San Francisco for treatment. This prohibited him from being a part of the battle of Midway. He said to a group of midshipman while in the US that "missing the battle of Midway has been the greatest disappointment of my career, but I am going back to the Pacific, where I intend personally to have a crack at those yellow-bellied sons of bitches and their carriers."

Upon Admiral Halsey's return to the Pacific by air to Noumea, New Caledonia, he was handed a sealed envelope containing a message from Admiral Nimitz saying, "You will take command of the South Pacific area and South Pacific forces immediately." Two days after taking command, he ordered all naval officers to dispense from wearing neckties. This order was given to conform to army practice but mostly for comfort in the tropics. With Admiral Halsey in command, the war in the Solomons' went on the offensive. His willingness to place at risk two of his fast battleships for a night engagement around Guadalcanal paid off with the navy winning the battle. These battles with the Japanese checked their offensive and drained their naval forces of carrier aircraft and experienced pilots. By this time in the war, the US Navy was doing things the Japanese never thought possible: neutralizing the Japanese land-based planes and dominating whatever area in which the fleet was operating.

At this point in the Pacific, the overall command was divided between Admirals Halsey and Spruance. Halsey self-dubbed his staff as the "department of dirty tricks." The two admirals were a contrast in styles. Halsey was aggressive and a risk-taker while Spruance was cautious, professional, and calculating. Most high-ranking officers preferred to serve under Spruance, while the common sailors preferred and were proud to serve under Halsey.

Eventually, Halsey passed the command of his fleet to Spruance. But in departing after the cessation of hostilities, his aggressive nature came through in a communiqué, which said three things:

- There is a cessation of hostilities.
- The war is over.
- But if any Japanese planes appear, shoot them down in a friendly way.

He was one of the few navy personnel who was able to work with General MacArthur, and he expressed the greatest admiration and respect for him.

The next section of the book describes the battles that took place in the Pacific Theater.

In the first six to twelve months of a war with the United States and Great Britain I will run wild and win victory upon victory. But then, if the war continues after that, I have no expectations of success.

—Admiral Isoroku Yamamoto, Commander in Chief of the Japanese Navy

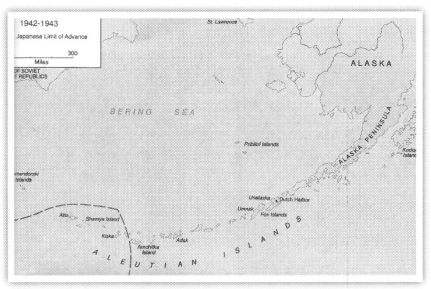

**The Aleutian Islands Adak, Attu, and Kiska
(Courtesy of US Army history public domain)**

The Japanese wanted to control the Aleutian Islands to prevent a possible US attack across the northern Pacific. The US was fearful that these islands could be used for an assault on the West Coast. The battle for the Aleutians has been referred to as the "forgotten battle" due to it being fought at the same time as the Guadalcanal Campaign. In both campaigns, the third enemy appeared, which was composed of the weather in the Aleutians and the jungle and swamps in Guadalcanal.

The Aleutian Campaign in early 1943 brought my ship, the USS J. Franklin Bell, to its first of many campaigns in the Pacific war. The USS J. Franklin Bell, with several other ships, arrived at Adak in the Aleutian Islands with D-day set for August 30, 1942. The occupation forces were prepared for enemy opposition, but the landing was accomplished without incident. The Japanese had withdrawn from Adak.

The attack on the island of Attu was quite difficult, because there was a shortage of landing craft, unsuitable beaches, and equipment that failed to work in the appalling weather conditions. Intermittent shelling of the beaches by the Japanese slowed the landing of supplies, and four narrow misses by enemy torpedoes did not enhance the Bell's unloading operation. Shipmate Bob Tagatz spent the first night in a LCVP command boat and had this to say about the Aleutian campaign:

> We landed on Adak with Seabees and Alaskan Scouts, no opposition. They were to build an airfield. We landed, on Attu May 11, 1943, with the Army 7th Infantry Division. Holtz Bay, northern side. Massacre Bay was the other landing, Southside. We could only land 4 LCVP's at a time. I was engineer F1/c; Jim Weaver, Coxan. We were the control LCVP with an Officer. We controlled the landing craft. Visibility: ship's length. Received

motor fire from across Holtz Bay. Japanese in a cave. Landed some shots as close as 20 yards from boat. Too close so we kept moving around.

The destroyer Phelps DD498 made a couple of runs with its 5-inch point blank and took care of the motor and Japanese. That evening a Japanese sub came out of Holtz Bay and fired a torpedo at the Bell which missed. The Bell took off leaving us in boats to find ways to stay alive. We had about 1500 troops ashore but didn't know if the Japanese would counterattack. I believe we lost 3 LCVP's because of load. We couldn't get to the bilge strainers to be cleaned. Boat sank but we transferred crew to another boat. We finally landed all the boats about 2 miles down the island. What a night: fog, rain, cold, didn't know if Japanese were coming, visibility zero. After all the men and supplies unloaded, we took on wounded to return to the States. To my surprise a man from my hometown Montello, Wisconsin, a Sergeant Phil Czeshleba came aboard. He was wounded by shell fragments as he was bringing a squad member back to his fox hole. He got the Silver Star for this. The J. Franklin Bell got back to San Francisco, California safely. Then on down to San Diego to Travis for the next landing which would be Kiska. On August 16, 1943, we landed the Fourth Army, but the Japanese were already gone.

Two members of the crew, Buck Jordon and Leroy Holland, were wounded during the landings. Leroy Holland did not survive the wounds and was buried at sea on May 17, 1943. Very applicable is another poem written by Tim Churchill.

Another Shipmate Gone

Another shipmate passed beyond,
The veil of life on earth,
Reminding us who still remain,
To value life from birth.

The past, and all that happened then,
Just makes us whom we are;
We learn to give, and take and love,
And wish on every star.

Each failure ends one more success,
No effort is in vain,
But wins and losses teach us well,
That sunshine follows rain.

We learn to take life's ebb and flow,
Like sweet and bitter times;
Maturity means bearing pain,
When good and bad combines.

Then having learned, we share life's load,
And share the love we give,
Then honor those whom we have loved,
And Value those who live.

On May 29, 1943, the last of the Japanese forces staged, without warning, one of the first and largest banzai attacks of the Pacific Campaign. After furious, brutal, often hand-to-hand bloody combat, the Japanese were virtually eliminated. Only twenty-eight men had been willing to be taken alive. The final activity in the Aleutians was the invasion of Kiska.

The J. Franklin Bell went to San Francisco to pick up the troops who were in training for the Kiska operation in early July 1943. Then the ship proceeded to the San Diego area to practice landing with other ships of the task group. Finally, the group proceeded to the Aleutians and anchored in Kulak Bay, Adak on August 5, 1943.

The troops were lowered away with full equipment for a week of conditioning in the Aleutian's terrain and weather. They returned to the ship on August 11, 1943. This training resulted from the bad judgment made in the Attu campaign of not having issued the soldiers heavy clothing while the Japanese were dressed in fur-lined uniforms. It should be noted that 2,100 of the 3,416 wounded for the entire Aleutian campaign were the result of exposure, trench foot, and shock. D-day for the Kiska invasion was set for August 15, 1943. The forces landed to find the island abandoned. Under the cover of favorable weather conditions and fog, the Japanese had removed their troops on July 28. The casualties still numbered 313 as a result of friendly fire, booby traps, and weather conditions. (See Table 2 on the next page.) As with Attu, Kiska offered an extremely hostile environment.

While many people in the US in 1943 were searching their world maps to locate places like Guadalcanal and the Aleutians Islands, on the home front, the Pentagon, the world's largest office building, was being completed. The average family wage per year was $2,000. We were made aware that the future President John F. Kennedy's PT boat 109 was sunk by a Japanese destroyer. A Coca Cola cost $0.05, and you could relax to Glen Miller's "In the Mood" or watch the young and not-so-young go crazy over the music of Frank Sinatra.

Table 2: Troop and ship casualties for the Aleutians Campaign

TROOPS	USA	JAPAN
Killed	1481	4350
Wounded	3416	0
Captured	8*	28
MISSING IN ACTION	640	0

* US Navy

SHIPS	USA		JAPAN	
	Destroyed	Damaged	Destroyed	Damaged
Submarines	2	-	-	-
Warships	-	-	7	-
Destroyers	1	-	-	-
Cargo Ships	-	-	9	-

THE SOLOMON ISLANDS AND NEW GUINEA CAMPAIGNS

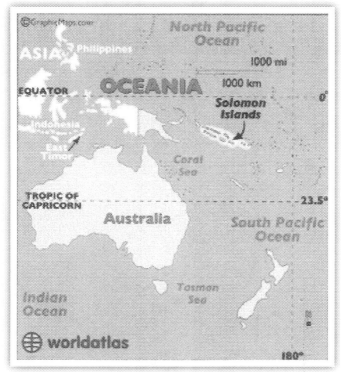

**The Solomon Islands and
Bougainville of New Guinea
(Courtesy of Worldatlas)**

It is difficult to separate these two battles during WWII, because they were fought at the same time under very similar conditions.

The struggle for New Guinea began with the Japanese capturing the city of Rabaul at the northeastern tip of the New Britain Island in January 1942. During the next year, the Japanese built up this area into a major air and naval base.

It is worth noting some basic facts that existed at the time these battles for the Solomon Islands and New Guinea were initiated. The timeframe was about seven to eight months after the attack on Pearl Harbor. The amount of training our troops received was limited for both enlisted men and officers. The conditions under which they had to fight were not like any condition they had ever encountered. Areas that were not waterlogged were either dense jungle or covered with dense patches of kunai grass which could grow to six feet tall with leaves that were wide and sharp. Temperatures in this grass could reach 122 degrees. The greatest disease that the troops faced was malaria. But other diseases, such as dengue fever, scrub typhus,

**A patrol pushes its way through thick kunai grass
(Courtesy of US Army public domain)**

dysentery from many sources, and fungal infections were common. The battle for the Solomons' was started during the tropical wet season. Lt. General Robert L. Eichelberger wrote, "At Buna that year it rained about a hundred and seventy inches." He went on to say that during December 1942 and January 1943, daily rainfall of eight to ten inches was not uncommon. Under these conditions, the limited tracks, seldom more than just footpaths, quickly became boggy.

Immediately after the attack on Pearl Harbor, the Japanese initiated attacks on Thailand, the Philippines, the American base on Guam, and Wake Island, including the British possessions of Malaya, Singapore, and Hong Kong. In March 1942, President Roosevelt ordered General MacArthur to formulate a defense plan with Australia. This was accomplished, and Prime Minister John Curtin agreed to place the Australian forces under MacArthur's command.

The Japanese never initially intended to invade Australia, because it was judged to be beyond the capability of the Japanese military. Instead, they adopted a strategy of isolating Australia from the United States. This was to include the capture and occupation of several locations, including Port Moresby in the Territory of New Guinea, Papua New Guinea, the Solomon Islands, Fiji, Samoa, and New Caledonia. However, in the battle of the Coral Sea, the Allies suffered a higher loss in ships. They did, however, achieve a crucial strategic victory by turning the Japanese landing force back. MacArthur understood the importance of Port Moresby and decided to build two airbases to protect it from the Japanese, one to the west in Australia controlled New Guinea and one to the east, which ended up being at Milne Bay.

The Coral Sea battle was considered a loss by the Japanese because the attempted invasion of Port Moresby was stopped. This caused the Japanese to have second thoughts, because up to this point, everything in the war was going Japan's way. It was difficult for the Japanese to admit defeat, so they continued their effort to take Port Moresby by landing troops by sea. These attempts were not successful due to an overwhelming buildup of US naval forces. In fact, the area became known as Iron Bottom Sound because so many ships were sunk in this area.

Since the Japanese controlled most of New Guinea, they decided to use a land approach to capture Port Moresby. This required that they use the Kokoda Track to cross the Owen Stanley Range. The Kokoda Track Campaign began with the Japanese establishing beachheads at Buna, Gona, and Sanananda. As this campaign was underway, the Japanese attempted to capture the strategically important Milne Bay area but were defeated. This was the first land defeat of the Japanese, and it raised the Allied morale across the Pacific Theater. Historian Samuel Eliot Morison revealed that the Australians were fighting mad after the battle of Milne Bay. He revealed the following: "Thenceforth, the battle of Milne Bay became an infantry struggle in the sopping jungle carried on mostly at night under pouring rain. The Aussies were fighting mad, for they had found some of their captured fellows tied to trees and bayoneted to death, surmounted by the placard, 'It took them a long time to die.'"

When the Japanese force had gotten within twenty miles of Port Moresby, they were ordered to halt the advance and return to their base. This change in plans was the result of Japanese loses in the battle at Guadalcanal, the strategic naval loss at Coral Sea, and the unbelievable naval loss at Midway. The Japanese general in charge of the Solomon Islands Campaign concluded that he did not have the resources to fight all the battles at the same time and ordered the troops to withdraw. The Japanese fought a well-ordered rear-guard action as they retreated across the Owen Stanley Range with the Australian forces in close pursuit. Historian Morison also had this to say about the Owen Stanley Range: "The Owen Stanley Range is a jagged, precipitous obstacle covered with tropical rainforest up to the pass at 6,500-foot elevation, and with moss like a thick wet sponge up to the highest peak, 13,000 feet above sea level. The Kokoda Trail was suitable for splay-toed aborigines but a torture to modern soldiers carrying heavy equipment."

Some areas in the Solomons' and New Guinea were bypassed, leaving the Japanese cut off from supply lines and therefore isolated. The large Japanese naval base at Rabaul on New Britain is one example. The Allied airpower prevented the Japanese from supplying food, supplies, and reinforcements for the troops at Rabaul. In the closing stages of the battle at Buna-Gona, significant numbers of the defenders were withdrawn by sea or escaped overland toward the Japanese base at Salamaua and Lae. The remaining garrison fought to the death, almost to the man.

The resolve and tenacity of the Japanese in defense was unprecedented and had not been previously encountered. It was a warning of things to come for the war in the Pacific.

 Patriotic poetry is written by Timothy D. Churchill (1926-2019). This book is in his Honor and Memory.

THE BATTLE OF GUADALCANAL

Guadalcanal
(Courtesy of Wikimedia - Free Media Repository)

The battle for Guadalcanal was among the first major offensives by the US in the Pacific. It was fought between August 1942 and February 1943. The reason for the delay in the offensive was that President Roosevelt and some military leaders had the opinion that Germany had to be defeated first. At the same time, other military commanders pointed out that if left unchecked, the Japanese would cut off all communication and supply lines between the US and Australia and New Zealand. Therefore, the need to put a stop to the Japanese advances to the East meant going on the offensive in the Pacific. This resulted in Guadalcanal, along with the Aleutian Campaign, being the beginning of the march toward Japan—the first rungs of the ladder.

Stretcher detail in the jungle of Guadalcanal
(Courtesy of National Archives public domain)

It was at this time that the US decided that it must select a long-term strategy. MacArthur was determined to keep his pledge of "I shall return" by directing the war through the Philippines while the naval commanders proposed a central Pacific route to Japan. In May 1943, the Joint Chiefs of Staff resolved the dispute between MacArthur and the navy by approving a "dual drive" toward Japan. Earlier, in August 1942, the Allied forces surprised the Japanese by landing and capturing Tulagi and Florida as well as an airfield on Guadalcanal.

The airfield was named Henderson Field after a marine pilot previously lost in combat at Midway. The Japanese made numerous attempts to retake the airfield but were never successful. On one attempt, the first wave of Japanese soldiers to breach the razor-sharp wire that was strung around the perimeter of the base threw themselves onto the wire so the second wave could cross over their bodies to breach the barrier.

The battle for Guadalcanal was costly to both sides in the war. The US suffered heavy losses in personnel during this campaign. The losses were of such magnitude that the US refused to release the numbers to the public. Likewise, the loss to the Japanese (both strategically and in manpower and materials) was enormous. About 25,000 experienced Japanese ground troops were killed during the campaign for Guadalcanal.

Author John Vader remarked about the fighting conditions, "In the swamp country which surrounded the area were large crocodiles. Incidence of malaria was almost one hundred per cent. At Sanananda were swamps and jungles with typhus-ridden crawling roots reaching out into stagnant pools infested with mosquitoes and numerous crawling insects. Every foxhole was filled with water and Thompson sub machine guns jammed with the gritty mud and were unreliable in the humid atmosphere."

THE STORY OF JACOB VOUZA ON GUADALCANAL

During the entire Solomon Island Campaign, the resourcefulness of the Australia Coastwatchers proved invaluable to the Allied cause. One example is the story of Jacob C. Vouza. Vouza was born in Tasimboko, Guadalcanal, and educated at the South Seas Evangelical Mission School. Upon his conversion to Christianity, he took the name of Jacob. In 1916, he joined the Solomon Islands Protectorate Armed Constabulary and retired after twenty-five years of service at the rank of sergeant major. After many attempts on his life from criminals he had arrested, he took retirement, and with his wife and two daughters, he moved back to Guadalcanal. He gained the attention of the US Marines by rescuing an aviator from the USS Wasp who was shot down in Japanese held territory. He guided the pilot to American lines, where he met the marines for the first time.

Vouza then volunteered to be a Coastwatcher and scout behind enemy lines for the US forces. On one of his missions, he came upon a group of soldiers, mistakenly thinking they were American. To get their attention, he waved a small US flag that had been given to him by a marine.

Unfortunately, it was a Japanese unit. He was captured and questioned about the marines' location and strength. Vouza was questioned for hours but refused to talk. The Japanese commander ordered him bayoneted to death because shooting would have given away their location. He was bayoneted in both arms, his throat, a shoulder, his face, and his stomach and left to die.

After his captors left the area, he freed himself by chewing through the ropes that the Japanese had used to bind him. He made his way through miles of jungle to the American lines. Before allowing medical attention, he briefed the marines on the Japanese force that was about to attack the marines. The warning gave the marines a brief but precious time before the Japanese attack. The subsequent Battle of the Tenaru was a victory for the marines.

He was then given sixteen pints of blood, and after spending twelve days in the hospital, he returned to duty as a scout.

Vouza was highly decorated for his service during WWII. He received a Silver Star, a Legion of Merit from the US, and the George Medal from the British as well as being knighted by the Queen of England.

THE STORY OF JOHN BASILONE (MEDAL OF HONOR AND NAVY CROSS)

John Basilone was born at his parents' home on November 4, 1916, in Buffalo, New York. He entered the army in 1934 and spent three years in the Philippines, where he obtained the nickname "Manila John." After retiring, he became a truck driver for a few years and then decided he wanted to go back to Manila. He chose to enlist in the marines, as he thought that would be the quickest way. However, the Japanese attack on Pearl Harbor resulted in him being sent to Guadalcanal.

In October 1942, during the battle for Henderson Field, his unit came under attack by about three thousand Japanese. Basilone was commander of two sections of machine guns that fought for two days to the point where he and two other marines were the only ones left. He then moved a new gun into position and continued to fire at the charging Japanese. Basilone then repaired another gun and held their defensive position until replacements arrived.

With the battle continuing, ammunition became low, and despite their supply lines being cut off by the enemy, Basilone fought through hostile areas to resupply his heavy machine gunners with the much-needed ammunition. When the last of the ammo ran out, Basilone held his position with a pistol and a machete. Private Nash Phillips recalls, "Basilone had a machine gun on the go for 3 days and nights without sleep, rest, or food. He was in a good emplacement and causing the Japanese a lot of trouble, not only from his machine gun, but also from his pistol." For this action, Basilone was awarded the Medal of Honor, which reads:

> **John Basilone,** born November 4, 1916 in Buffalo, New York. While the enemy was hammering at the marines' defensive position, Basilone, in charge of two sections of heavy machine guns, fought valiantly to check the savage and determined assault. He repaired a gun under fire and then manned it gallantly, holding his line until a replacement arrived. A little later, with ammunition critically low and supply lines cut off, Sgt. Basilone, at great risk of his own life and in face of continued enemy attack, battled his way through hostile lines with urgently needed shells for his gunners. The result was a virtual annihilation of a Japanese regiment. He is also the only enlisted man to have received both the Medal of Honor and the Navy Cross.

In 1943, Basilone returned to the US and participated in war bond tours. During this tour, he met his wife, Lena Mae Riggi. They were married on July 10, 1944.

Basilone was not comfortable among the politicians, celebrities, and national press and requested a return to duty, which was denied. He was offered a commission and an assignment as an instructor, both of which he turned down.

His second request for active duty was accepted, and on February 19, 1945, he was in the D-day landing on Iwo Jima.

The Japanese had built heavy fortified blockhouses throughout the island. It was from one of these blockhouses that his unit had been pinned down. Basilone made his way around the side of the Japanese position until he was directly above the blockhouse. With demolitions and grenades, he single handedly destroyed the blockhouse and the Japanese troops inside.

In his march toward Airfield Number 1, he came upon a marine tank that was trapped in an enemy mine field. Under heavy enemy fire from mortar and artillery, Basilone led the tank out of the hazard area to safety.

Sadly, as he approached the airfield, he was killed by mortar shrapnel. However, research by Hugh Ambrose for the miniseries *The Pacific* said that he was killed from small arms fire. The results were the same in either case.

For his actions at Iwo Jima, he was awarded the marines' highest honor, the Navy Cross.

THE STORY OF CALVIN GRAHAM DURING NAVAL BATTLE GUADALCANAL

Another bizarre story about World War II is that of Calvin Graham, who enlisted in the navy shortly after Pearl Harbor. He joined the USS South Dakota. During a naval battle at Guadalcanal, he helped in the fire control efforts during battle aboard his ship. For his efforts, he was awarded the Bronze Star and the Purple Heart. When his mom revealed his age, he was put in the brig for three months for lying about it. When his sister threatened to go to the newspaper with his story, he was released with a dishonorable discharge and stripped of his medals for lying about his age. Later, he joined the marines and ended up breaking his back, only to spend the rest of his life fighting for medical benefits and cleaning up his record. After writing to Congress in 1988, he was given back all his medals except the Purple Heart. By the way, he was twelve years old when he first enlisted in the navy.

THE BATTLE FOR NEW GEORGIA

The Imperial Japanese Army believed the Solomon Islands would be lost, and they decided to make their defensive stand at Bougainville because it would be much easier to supply and reinforce. At the same time, Japan prepared for an attack on New Georgia by landing 10,500 troops and nine thousand troops on an adjacent island of Kolombangara, which was part of the New Georgia group. They were well entrenched and waiting for the Allied attack.

The Allied base on Guadalcanal continued to suffer from Japanese air raids. The Japanese air base at Munda in New Georgia territory provided a refueling stop for planes from the Japanese base at Rabaul. The Allies attempted to make the base unusable by repeated bombing and shelling. But the Japanese were always quick with repairs. The Allies then decided to take Munda Air Base by ground troops. Because New Georgia was in the South Pacific area, the operation would be under the command of Admiral William F. Halsey. On-the-ground leaders were Major General Oscar W. Griswold, commander of the XIV Army Corps, and General Hester.

The battle for New Georgia was not going very well, so Admiral Halsey sent Lieutenant General Millard F. Harmon to investigate. Harmon gave field command to Major General Oscar W. Griswold so that General Hester could concentrate on leading his own division. Historian Samuel Eliot Morison had this to say about conditions at that time in New Georgia:

Darkness came to the jungle like the click of a camera shutter. Then the Japanese crept close to the American lines. They attacked with bloodcurdling screams, plastered bivouacs with artillery and mortar barrages, crawled silently into American foxholes and stabbed or strangled the occupants. Often, they cursed in English, rattled their equipment, named the American commanding officers and dared the Americans to fight, reminding them that they were "not in the Louisiana maneuvers now." For the sick and hungry soldiers who had fought all day, this unholy shivaree was terrifying. They shot at everything in sight- fox fire on rotting stumps, land crabs clattering over rocks, even comrades.

Under a change in leadership, the Americans went on the offensive. The Japanese attempted to bring reinforcements and sent three ships loaded with troops. However, they were met with six US destroyers under the command of Commander Frederick Mooseburger and sunk. The one Japanese escort ship did not linger to look for survivors. The Japanese leader did his best to hold the islands to give the northern Solomons' time to get reinforcements.

There are many other smaller battles which have not been mentioned, such as the battle of Savo Island, Buna, Gona, etc. Each of these battles is reviewed separately because of the intensity of these battles and the need to recognize the forgotten warriors who fought under the most difficult conditions in the Pacific Theater of war.

THE BATTLE OF SAVO ISLAND

The Battle of Savo Island was fought on August 8–9, 1943. This was the first major naval engagement of the Guadalcanal campaign, and so many ships were sunk in the area that it became to be known as Iron Bottom Sound. The Imperial Japanese Navy (IJN), in response to the allied landings on the eastern part the Solomon Islands, put together a naval force to interrupt the landing group. In night action (in which the Japanese had trained), the IJN force thoroughly surprised the Allied force. The battle has often been described as the worst defeat in a fair fight in the history of the United States Navy. The fact that it was fought at night ended up favoring the Americans, because the IJN, fearing the US carriers would spot them at daybreak, did not follow through and destroy Allied invasion transports. They did, however, interrupt the unloading of equipment and supplies. This battle was the first of five costly battles fought in support of our troops who had been placed on Guadalcanal. It was also costly in ships and casualties, as the Allied forces lost 1,077 troops, with the IJN losing only 129.

THE BATTLE OF BUNA-GONA

This battle was fought between November 1942 and January 1943. As noted, operations were severely impacted by terrain, climate, disease, and a lack of infrastructure. These conditions had a major influence on the conventional Allied doctrine of maneuver and firepower. During the early stages of this battle, the US soldiers faced a severe shortage of food and ammunition. Also, the battle exposed serious problems with suitability and performance of the Allied equipment. These factors were compounded by repeat demands from General MacArthur for a rapid conclusion to the battle. He was somewhat unaware of the conditions that his troops were facing. Terrain and persistent pressure for haste meant little (if any) time for reconnaissance. As an example of MacArthur's attitude, he placed Lt. General Eichelberger in charge of the US 32nd Infantry with orders to remove all officers who would not fight and replace them with sergeants if necessary. MacArthur said to Eichelberger, "I want you to take Buna or not come back alive." All of this was said from the comfort of his command post in Melbourne, Australia.

The following is a list of men awarded the Medal of Honor for their actions in the battles of Guadalcanal, Buna-Gona, New Georgia, and Salvo Island. (To read the citations of all listed, go to _www.themedalofhonor.org_.) In some cases, the detailed description of the citation is unique, and I have included it for the convenience of the reader.

Kenneth D. Bailey, born October 26, 1910, in Pawnee, Oklahoma

John Basilone, born November 4, 1916, in Buffalo, New York

Harold William Bauer, born November 20, 1908, in Woodruff, Kansas

George W. G. Boyce Jr., born in New York City, New York

Elmer J. Burr, born in Neenah, Wisconsin

Anthony Casamento, born November 16, 1920, in Brooklyn, New York

Daniel Judson Callaghan, born July 26, 1982, in San Francisco, California

Dale Eldon Christensen, born in Cameron Township, Iowa

Charles W. Davis, born February 21, 1917, in Gordo, Alabama

Merritt Austin Edson, born April 25, 1897, in Rutland, Vermont

Gerald L. Endl, born in Ft. Atkinson, Wisconsin

Ray E. Eubanks, born February 6, 1922, in Snow Hill, North Carolina

Joseph Jacob Foss, born April 17, 1915, in Sioux Falls, South Dakota

William G. Fournier, born June 21, 1913, in Norwich, Connecticut

Kenneth E. Gruennert, born in Helenville, Wisconsin

Johnnie David Hutchins, born on August 4, 1922, in Weimer, Texas

Lewis Hall, born Mach 2, 1895, in Bloom, Ohio

Neel E. Kearby, born in Wichita Falls, Texas

Donald R. Logaugh, born in Freeport, Pennsylvania

Bruce McCandless, born August 12, 1911, in Washington, District of Columbia

Douglas Albert Munro, born October 11, 1919, in Vancouver, British Columbia, Signalman First Class, US Coast Guard. Munro exhibited extraordinary heroism and conspicuous gallantry in action. After making preliminary plans for the evacuation of nearly five hundred beleaguered marines, Petty Officer Munro, under constant strafing by enemy machine guns on the island and at great risk of his life, daringly led five of his small craft toward the shore. As he closed the beach, he signaled the others to land, and then to draw the enemy fire and protect the heavy-laden boats, he valiantly placed his craft with its two small guns as a shield between the beach and the Japanese. When the perilous task of evacuation was nearly completed, Munro was instantly killed by enemy fire, but his crew, two of whom were wounded, carried on until the last troops had loaded and cleared the beach. He is the only Coast Guard person to receive the Medal of Honor.

Robert Allen Owens, born September 13, 1920, in Greenville, South Carolina

Frank J. Petrarca, born in Cleveland, Ohio

Robert S. Scott, born in Washington, District of Columbia

Norman Scott, born August 10, 1889, in Indianapolis, Indiana

Herbert Emery Schonland, born September 7, 1900, in Portland, Maine

Junior Van Noy, born in Grace, Idaho

Rodger W. Young, born in Tiffin, Ohio

Table 4: Troop casualties for the battle of Guadalcanal Island

TROOP	USA	JAPAN	OTHER
Killed	727	18,500-21,500	516*
Wounded	-	-	-
Captured	-	-	-

* Australia Troops

SHIP/ AIRCRAFT	USA		JAPAN	
	Destroyed	Damaged	Destroyed	Damaged
Ships	29	-	38	-
Aircraft	615	-	683-880	-

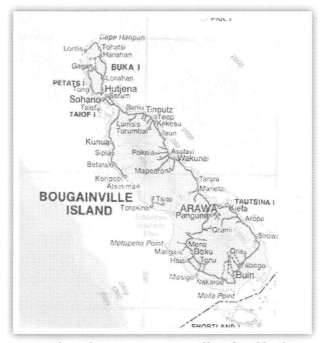

**Before the war, Bougainville Island had
been administered by Australia as a part
of New Guinea territory, even though
geographically a part of the Solomon Islands
(Courtesy of Wikimedia Commons
Free Media Repository)**

The Bougainville battle started in 1943 and was fought by the
Allies to retake the island that the Japanese had occupied in
1942. The Japanese had developed naval aircraft bases in the
north, east, and south of the island plus airfields and naval
anchorages on the adjacent islands of Treasury and Shortland.
The Japanese purpose of these military facilities was to
protect Rabaul, the major Japanese garrison and naval base
in New Guinea, as well as on down the Solomon Island chain

to Guadalcanal. They also constructed airfields and naval anchorages on the adjacent islands of Treasury and Shortland.

Before the war, Bougainville had been administered as part of the Australian territory of New Guinea, even though geographically, Bougainville is part of the Solomon Island chain. Thus, the US began fighting alongside the Australians. That is why Australian casualties have begun to be listed on the tables.

The Royal Australian Navy had set up a remarkable means of communication as far back as 1919 in what they called Coastwatchers. This was a group of individuals—missionaries, farmers, traders, and the like—who reported anything unusual along the coast. It was through this effort that in 1939, the Australians became aware of the special interest Japan was making in the Solomon Island area, and as a result, they expanded the Coastwatchers' effort on several Islands.

The Coastwatchers were not to confront the enemy but rather to fade into the jungle and keep reporting on a special radio frequency that was constantly monitored. Through these resources, advanced warning would come on air attacks that gave information on the type of plane, number, and direction, thereby allowing time for anti-aircraft crews to be ready for the enemy attack.

Combat operations on Bougainville ended with the surrender of the Japanese forces on August 21, 1945, which consisted of about 23,500 Japanese troops and laborers.

The written descriptions of the battles for Guadalcanal and Bougainville do not come close to describing the intensity of these battles and the terrain and conditions under which the US and the Australian troops had to cope while facing a fanatical enemy. Remember, these troops who fought in the Solomon Islands were America's very first WWII combat troops. The officers who led them were also rookies in combat. It was on-the-job training in warfare that meant life or death for everyone in a jungle that is hard to describe with its swamp-invested critters and insects. On top of that, they fought against an enemy hellbent on dying before surrendering. These soldiers deserve our highest praise and should never be forgotten.

THE STORY OF ADMIRAL ISOROKU YAMAMOTO

Another reason for remembering Bougainville is that it deals with the admiral who had the greatest influence on the surprise attack on Pearl Harbor. To boost morale following the defeat at Guadalcanal, Admiral Yamamoto decided to visit troops on an island off the coast of Bougainville on April 18, 1943. Naval intelligence had learned of his planned flight. President Roosevelt, after receiving this information, ordered Secretary of Navy Frank Knox to "get to Yamamoto." Admiral Nimitz, after consulting with Admiral Halsey, authorized the mission. On April 17, P-38 Lightning aircraft were selected to be the transport because they were the only fighter planes with enough range. Select pilots from three different units were informed they were intercepting "an important person" with no specific name given.

The sixteen P-38 intercepted the Japanese planes over Bougainville, and a dogfight ensued. There is some doubt as to who shot down Yamamoto's plane, as Lt. Rex Barber and Lt. Thomas Lamphier have each made claim to the event. The second plane carrying Yamamoto's staff was also shot down but managed to crash into the sea with two survivors to tell their story. Lt. Barber remembers seeing the plane with smoke coming from it as it crashed into the jungle. Lt. Lamphier remembers shooting off the right wing and then seeing it crash into the jungle. Yamamoto's body was found the next day by a Japanese search party. His body was thrown from the plane but landed still upright under a tree near the crash site. It was said that his head was slumped over as if he were taking a nap.

A postmortem of the body disclosed that he had received two 50-caliber bullet wounds, one to the back and another to the face that exited above his left eye. The Japanese doctor said the head wound was the cause of death.

Table 5: Troop casualties for the Bougainville Campaign

TROOPS	USA	JAPAN	AUSTRALIAN
Killed	727	18,500-21,500	516
Wounded	-	-	572
Captured	-	-	-

The following five troop members were awarded the Medal of Honor for their actions at Bougainville. For a detailed description on why they were awarded this medal, go to *www.themedalofhonor.org.*

Jesse R. Drowley, born September 9, 1919, in St. Charles, Michigan

Henry Gurke, born November 6, 1922, in Neche, North Dakota

Robert Murray Hanson, born February 4, 1920, in Lucknow, India

Robert Allen Owens, born October 11, 1919, in Vancouver, British Columbia

Herbert Joseph Thomas, born February 8, 1918, in Columbus, Ohio

THE BATTLE OF JAVA SEA

**The first and second battle of the Java Sea
(Courtesy of Wikimedia Commons,
the free media repository)**

The Japanese invasion of Indonesia and the rest of the Dutch East Indies proceeded at a rapid pace. Troop convoys, protected by escorting cruisers and destroyers, were on their way in February 1942 to occupy the islands. To defend the islands, a joint effort American, British, Dutch, and Australian Command (ABDACOM) was formed under the command of US Admiral Thomas C. Hart. The joint force consisted of two heavy and three light cruisers and nine destroyers. They faced the Japanese force, which had two heavy and two light cruisers and fourteen destroyers protecting troop ships with personnel to land and occupy the islands. The Allied goal was to get to the troop ships. But the Japanese firepower was much more powerful than out vintage WWI guns. Also, the Japanese had air power for support.

The combined striking force made several attempts to reach the Japanese troop convoy, but each effort was met with a more powerful Japanese Navy. The Dutch strike force commander, Rear Admiral Karel Doorman, went down with his flagship De Ruyter. The Dutch ship Java was also sunk at the same time. Only 111 sailors were saved from both ships.

The second Java Sea naval battle occurred the next day as the badly damaged HMS Exeter was heading for Ceylon for repairs and was being escorted by the HMS Encounter and the USS Pope. They were intercepted by a large Japanese force. Exeter and Encounter were sunk almost immediately. The Pope escaped but was attacked and sunk by an aerial attack a few hours later.

THE BATTLE OF THE CORA SEA

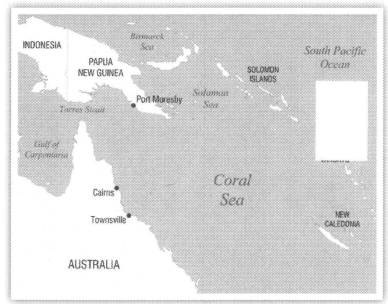

**The battle of Coral Sea, where the Japanese were
stopped from advancing across southeast Asia
(Courtesy of GNU free documentation Wikimedia)**

The battle of the Coral Sea was fought during May 1942. The Japanese, to strengthen their defensive position for their new empire in the South Pacific, decided they needed to occupy Port Moresby in New Guinea and Tulagi in the southeastern Solomon Islands. The US learned of the Japanese plan through signal intelligence and sent two US carrier task forces to oppose the Japanese offensive.

It should be noted that under the leadership of Navy Lt. Comdr. Joseph Rochefort, a person fluent in the Japanese language, the Japanese code was broken. This permitted Adm. Nimitz to know where the ships of the Japanese Navy were located and their intentions.

With knowledge of the Japanese invasions, two US Navy carrier task forces and a joint Australian-American cruiser force were sent to oppose the Japanese offensive. However, the Japanese were successful in the invasion of Tulagi, but many of their warships and aircraft were surprised by planes from the USS Yorktown. The Japanese, now aware of the US presence in the area, entered the Coral Sea with the intention to find and destroy the Allied naval forces. At this time, the Japanese Navy was far superior to the US Navy as a result of the losses they inflicted at Pearl Harbor. So, the US had to pick and choose where and when to engage in battle. The information derived from breaking the Japanese code allowed this to happen.

In early May, the two carrier forces exchanged airstrikes over a period of two days. The heavy losses in aircraft by the Japanese made them call off the invasion of Port Moresby for the time being.

Although a tactical victory for the Japanese in terms of ships sunk, the battle would prove to be a strategic victory for the US for the following reasons. This was the first time an expansion by the Japanese had been stopped. Additionally, two Japanese fleet carriers were out of action for the time being. One was damaged, and the other was depleted of its aircraft and would not be available in a month for the battle of Midway. This contributed significantly to the US victory in the battle of Midway.

Table 6: Troop, ship, and aircraft casualties for the Cora Sea naval battle

TROOP	USA	JAPAN
Killed	656	966
Wounded	-	-
Captured	-	-

*Australian Casualties

SHIP/ AIRCRAFT	USA		Japan	
	Destroyed	Damaged	Destroyed	Damaged
Fleet-carrier	1	1	1	1
Destroyer	1	-0	1	-0
War Ships	-	-	3	2
Transport	-	-	-	1
Oiler	1	-	-	-
Aircraft	69	0	92	0

The following three troop members were awarded the Medal of Honor for action during the naval battle of Cora Sea. (For a detailed description of why these men were awarded the medal, go to _www.themedalofhonor.org_.)

William E. Hall, born October 31, 1913, in Storrs, Utah
John J. Powers, born July 13, 1912, in New York City, New York
Milton E. Ricketts, born August 5, 1913, in Baltimore, Maryland

THE BATTLE FOR MIDWAY, THE TURNING POINT IN WORLD WAR II

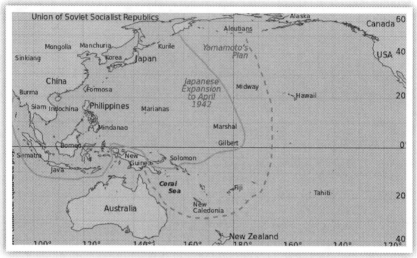

**The battle of Midway, where the US
achieved a miraculous naval victory
(Courtesy of Jacqueline Goins Bartek)**

Leading up to the naval battle of Midway was the battle of Java Sea, which the Japanese won handily. This caused the dissolvement of the ABDA (American British Dutch Australia) command. Then there was the tactical defeat at the battle of Coral Sea just one month before the battle at Midway. How prepared was the US? Remember, this was just six months after the attack on Pearl Harbor, and we were flying obsolete aircraft. Most of the pilots were rookies, such as Richard E. Fleming, who had arrived at Midway ten days after Pearl Harbor. The rookie pilots were called upon to fight a group of veteran Japanese pilots who were experienced in air battles and who had a fighter plane, the zero, that was far superior to our fighter aircraft at that time.

The Japanese plan was to lure the US aircraft carriers into a trap and to occupy Midway as a plan to extend their defensive perimeter. However, the US codebreakers were able to determine the date and location of the attack, enabling the US to set up an ambush of its own. The codebreakers were led by Joseph Rochefort, whose group determined that the code for Midway by the Japanese was AF. To confirm, Capt. Edwin Layton (Nimitz Chief of Intelligence Officer) asked Rochefort to send out an encoded message that said, "The water plant had failed on Midway, and there was a shortage of fresh water."

The code group soon received a message in Japanese that said the "AF was short on water." Adm. Nimitz now knew for sure the Japanese fleet was headed for Midway. The codebreaking crew was so accurate that they predicted the Japanese fleet would be within 175 miles of Midway at 6:00 a.m. on June 4 from a bearing 315° northwest. Adm. Nimitz's comments to Capt. Layton later were, "Well, you were only five miles, five degrees, and five minutes off."

The USS Yorktown was damaged in the Battle of the Coral Sea. It was thought that she would have to go to Puget Sound Naval Yard for several months of repair. But instead, the ship was taken to Pearl Harbor Naval Shipyard. After inspecting the ship and the damages, Adm. Nimitz said to the workers, "You have got three days to make the repairs." As a result, workers put her in a battle-ready condition in seventy-two hours, and off she went to fight in the battle of Midway.

During this campaign, three American servicemen (Ensign Wesley Osmus, Ensign Frank O'Flaherty, and Aviation Machinist Mate Bruno Gaido) were rescued from the sea by the Japanese. They were interrogated and then murdered by being tied to gasoline cans filled with water and thrown overboard.

The battle of Midway has been called the turning point of the Pacific. But the US did not move from a state of parity to a state of supremacy until after several more months of hard combat. However, it was the first major victory, and the Japanese military went to great lengths to hide the fact from their people. For example, they put their wounded in isolation and shipped them off to other areas of combat when they recovered without allowing them to see family or friends. It is more likely that the combined battles of the Coral Sea and Midway were the turning points in the Pacific war.

We should never forget what this group of pilots contributed toward the defeat of the Japanese. They did it within six months after Pearl Harbor. So, they did not have time to train. It was on-the-job training in an activity that meant life or death.

THE STORY OF RICHARD FLEMING, A MARINE PILOT AT MIDWAY

Richard Fleming was one of these pilots. He was born in St. Paul, Minnesota, and graduated from the University of Minnesota. When he finished school, he decided to try for flight training with the Marine Corps. During this time in Minnesota, he met Peggy Crooks at the local drugstore and began dating her.

But soon, it was off to Pensacola, Florida, for serious flight training.

Then, ten days after Pearl Harbor, he led his Marine Scout Bombing Squadron 1,137 miles across the Pacific to build up the defenses at Midway. In late May 1942, they received sixteen SDB-2 (Dauntless Dive Bombers), which were a great improvement over the Vindicators they had been flying. Training on the new planes was limited, because the Japanese fleet was on its way to Midway. On June 4, while flying wing on squadron, CO Major Lofton Henderson Japanese carriers were spotted, and at about the same time, Fleming shouted over the radio, "Here come the zeros." One of the first planes to be hit was Henderson, and as his plane went down Fleming took charge of the action.

His gunner was wounded but continued to fight off the zeros as Fleming flew through a hail of bullets from the zeros and anti-aircraft fire from the carriers. For greater accuracy, he flew to just over four hundred feet before dropping his bombs. When Fleming arrived back at the base, they counted 179 holes in his aircraft. He only had two minor wounds. (At this time in the war in the Pacific, the zero was the best fighter plane. But by the time of the battle of the Philippine Sea, the US had developed the F6F Hellcat, which was more powerful and maneuverable than the zero.)

The next day, Fleming was back in action, this time leading a flight of six SB2U-3s (carrier and land-based dive bombers). The target was the heavy cruiser Mikuma. The Japanese put up a strong defense, and Fleming, unable to use a true dive-bombing approach, decided to try a glide bombing run starting at four thousand feet and with the sun to his back. With smoke and fire seen in his engines, he managed to control his plane and drop his bombs. But when he pulled out of his glide, his plane burst into flames, and neither he nor his gunner Pfc. George A. Toms were ever seen again.

He had written a letter to his girlfriend Peggy Crooks on May 30, 1942, which was labeled, "To be opened only upon my death." The letter said, "Letters like this should not be morbid nor maudlin, and we'll let it suffice to say that I've been prepared for this rendezvous for some time. This is something that comes once to all of us and we can only bow before it." Richard E. Fleming was awarded the Medal of Honor for his actions in the battle of Midway. The following is the citation for Fleming.

> **Richard E. Fleming,** for extraordinary heroism and conspicuous intrepidity during action against enemy Japanese forces in the battle of Midway in June 1942, when his squadron

commander was shot down during the initial attack upon an enemy aircraft carrier. Captain Fleming led the remainder of the division with such fearless determination that he dived his plane to a perilously low altitude of four hundred feet before releasing his bomb. Although his plane was riddled with 179 hits, he pulled out with only two minor wounds. The following day, after fewer than four hours of sleep, he led the squadron in a coordinated attack against a Japanese battleship, during which his plane was set afire. He continued his attack to an altitude of five hundred feet, scored a near miss, and then crashed into the sea. This above is the official version, because there is reason to believe that he could have crashed his plane into the Japanese heavy cruiser Mikuma. This is based on eyewitness accounts by a Japanese naval officer and Fleming's wingman. But the story was never accepted by the Navy.

THE STORY OF GEORGE GAY'S SURVIVAL
DURING THE BATTLE FOR MIDWAY

But the battle was not without some heartbreaking events for the US. For example, from the carrier *Hornet,* Lt. Comdr. John Waldron led his squadron of fifteen planes and thirty men in their TBD-1 devastator planes (fighter planes) to attack the Japanese carriers, and only one, Lt. George Gay, survived. He survived the crash in the middle of the Japanese fleet and then survived the Japanese gunners by pulling a cushion over his head in the water to hide from Japanese ships that were in the area, strafing everything that moved. The Japanese ships came so close to him that he could see their faces. He was a witness to the sinking of three Japanese carriers and spent thirty hours in the water while the Japanese fleet moved away. He was then rescued by a navy PBY plane. After his navy career ended, George Gay spent thirty years as a commercial pilot for TWA. He passed away at seventy-seven, and his wife fulfilled his wishes. He was cremated, and his ashes were spread over the Midway battle area, as he wanted to join his comrades who did not survive the battle.

The *Hornet* sent twenty-eight other planes into this battle; only ten returned. The carrier *Yorktown* sent twenty-four planes into battle; only three returned. These men who fought for our country during this period and should never be forgotten. They fought without the benefit of the best in weapons, planes, and training that were available for later troops. Military historian John Keegan called it "the most stunning and decisive blow in the history of naval warfare." They turned defeat into victory for the US. And for their courage in battle, we are still speaking English in our country.

Above all, they should be placed on a pedestal for everyone to see, but after seventy-three years, they fall into the category of nearly forgotten warriors. I use the word *nearly* because of Hollywood director John Ford and his group of photographers on board one of the carriers during the battle. This allowed Ford to record most of the battles on camera, and Ford produced the film *The Battle of Midway*. Otherwise, the battle could fall into the category of battles like Tarawa, Tinian, Peleliu, etc. and be totally forgotten by now. Walter Lords, in his book on Midway in 1967, stated, "They had no right to win but they did." Ford also produced a documentary of the battle *(Torpedo Squadron),* which when seen by President Roosevelt. He ordered a copy for all mothers whose sons fought in the battle of Midway.

By the time of the battle of the Philippine Sea, the Japanese had somewhat rebuilt their carrier forces in terms of numbers, but their planes were obsolescent, and they had lost their veteran pilots to the war. Their planes were then being flown by inexperienced and poorly trained pilots. Also, their ability to build additional carriers was very poor compared to that of the US. For example, in the time it took the Japanese to build three carriers, the US had commissioned more than two dozen fleet, light fleet carriers, and numerous escort carriers.

Table 7: Troop, ship, and aircraft casualties that occurred during the naval battle of Midway

TROOP	USA	JAPAN
Killed	307	3057
Wounded	500	-
Captured	4*	-

*Captured, interrogated, and then murdered by the Japanese

Nation	USA		JAPAN	
	Destroyed	Damaged	Destroyed	Grounded
Carriers	1	-	4	-
Destroyer	1	-	-0	-
Heavy Cruiser	-	-	1	1
Aircraft	150	-	248	-

Only one Medal of Honor for action in the naval battle of Midway was awarded.

Richard E. Fleming, born November 2, 1917, in Saint Paul, Minnesota.

Casualties many; Percentage of dead not known; combat efficiency; we are winning.

—Colonel David M. Shoup (Tarawa, November 21, 1943)

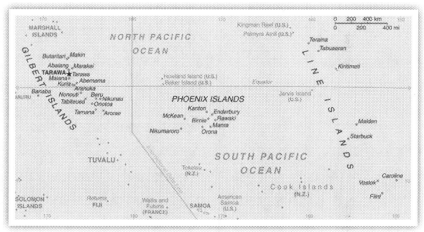

The island of Tarawa (upper left), where two out of three marines were killed in their attempt to establish a beachhead (Courtesy of Roman Catholic Church of Tarawa, public domain)

The battle for Tarawa in the Gilbert Islands was fought during the month of November 1943 and was the first amphibious landing into Japanese resistance in the march toward Japan. The previous landing in the Solomon Islands had seen little or no Japanese resistance in landing troops. It was the navy philosophy at the time of the war with Japan that for an amphibious attack to succeed, land-based aircraft were needed to protect the invasion force as well as to weaken the existing enemy defenses. This led to a ladder philosophy, with every move across the Pacific calculated to move up the rung of the ladder one step at a time. At that point in time, the Marianas was the major goal, but to get there, a base was needed in the Marshal Islands. To get to the Marshals, the airbase on the tiny island of Betio in the Tarawa Atoll had to be taken by the US.

Unfortunately, the Japanese had anticipated that the US would invade this island and had gone to great lengths to make an invasion impossible. It was reported that the Japanese commander on the island told his troops that "It would take one million men one hundred years to conquer Tarawa."

On November 1, 1943, my ship, the USS J. Franklin Bell loaded 1,800 officers and men of the 2nd Marine Division and departed for Efate, in the New Hebrides, where several practice landings were made. After this training, the Bell and other ships of the task force sailed for Tarawa on November 13. The force arrived off Tarawa Atoll just after midnight.

Early the next morning, the Japanese shore batteries opened fire on the Bell and other ships of the task force with a few narrow misses. So, the ships in the area withdrew outside the gun range.

After some delay, the H-hour was set for 0900. The assault troops in the amphibious tractor made it over the reef, but the LCVPs could not make it over, because the Higgins boats required five feet of clearance, and there were only four feet available. It was obvious the Marine planners had not planned for a neap tide, which occurs twice a month when the moon is near its first or last quarter. Neap tide is a phenomenon when the countering tug of the sun counteracts the pull of the moon, and water levels deviate less. Some observers noted that it seemed that "the water just sat there."

My nephew, Earl Hutchison, was among those who charged the beach. He said the water level was over his head, and he had to bounce up and down to get a breath of air. In full battle dress, that was becoming more and more difficult. He reached the point where he prayed to himself, "Lord, you are going to have to help me." Immediately, his feet felt the earth under his feet, and his mouth was above water level. He was a machine gunner, and with an assistant, he operated a BAR (Browning Automatic Rifle). He later told about the bonsai charges by the Japanese and how it seemed that the more you killed, the more they came. One Japanese soldier made it to their foxhole, but the enemy was killed in hand-to-hand combat. He himself was wounded when a bullet lodged in his head, so near the brain that physicians considered it better that he lived with bullet rather than chance an operation. The result was occasional headaches the rest of his life. He was awarded the Purple Heart and went back to Hawaii for rest and recuperation. Then, he went on to the battle for Tinian, where we came within a few feet of seeing each other.

At about 1750 hours on D-day, the Bell beach party left to report to the Commander of *Transport Four,* who was Captain McGovern, our previous ship's captain. The beach party worked all night under heavy enemy fire, salvaging stranded boats and unloading ammunition, water, and rations for the marines. During the night, casualties started arriving from the beach and continued for several days.

Orders were received by the Bell on the next day, November 21, to land her troops on the island of Bairiki, which was next to the island of Betio. This action was to block the Japanese troops from crossing a sandbar on the extreme eastern end of the islet to Bairiki. The landing came under machine gun fire, and the air force was called in to soften the defenders. The Japanese had gasoline stored in the bunker, which was ignited by the bombing and completely wiped out the bunker. The operation proceeded with little resistance. After the landing, unloading operations started and continued until late morning the following day. The next day, *Bell* returned to the transport area and continued to receive casualties from the ongoing battle on Betio. The lesson learned from this battle was of tremendous value to US planning for the rest of the war in the Pacific. However, it was costly, as two out of three marines did not survive the assault.

Another lesson was learned by mishaps such as transports missing the correct landing area; misjudging the depth of the tide, which resulted in the troops having to wade ashore under heavy enemy fire; and failure in coordinating air support, all of which proved tremendously valuable in the continued push across the Pacific.

Robert Sherrod, *Time* magazine war correspondent, wrote on December 6, 1943, that, "Last week some 2000 or 3000 United States Marines, most of them dead or wounded gave the nation a name to stand beside those of Concord Bridge, the Bonhomme

Richard, the Alamo, Little Bighorn and Belleau Wood. That name was Tarawa." That notoriety has not happened, but it should have—so, just one more reason for writing this book. My shipmate Clyde Crammond remembered his time on the Bell and *Tarawa*. He writes,

> I was only on the Bell for one invasion which was Tarawa so there is not much I can tell you that the others haven't already told you. I was an RM/3C at that time, so I was in the radio shack working 4 hours on and 4 hours off copying Morse code which came over in 5 letter code groups that were broadcasted by shore stations. When the Bell got back to Pearl Harbor, I was transferred to the 5th Amphibious Force Pacific which I stayed in the rest of my time in the Pacific.
>
> Control communications teams were being formed to coordinate troops and supplies at landing sites and I was in the first that was formed which consisted of a Chief Radio Repairman and 4 Radiomen. We were on small vessels such as PC, PCS and the like and were 1000 yards off the landing beach. All the troops in the landing craft were on the line of departure and we gave them the signal when to proceed. The Commodore was on board and gave the signal which one of them gave to all the landing craft on the circuit. Our first test was Kwajalein followed by Eniwetok and a total of 11 before the last one which was Okinawa.

Table 8: Troop and carrier causalities that occurred at Tarawa

TROOP	USA	JAPAN
Killed	1,711	4690
Wounded	2,100	-
Captured	-	17*

*129 Japanese Labors Captured (mostly Korean)

CARRIER	USA		JAPAN	
	Destroyed	Damaged	Destroyed	Damaged
Aircraft Carrier	1*	-	-	-

*The *Liscome Bay* (Dorie Miller's Ship) sunk with the loss of 687 shipmates

The following four troop members were awarded the Medal of Honor for action in the battle for Tarawa. For a detailed description on why the award was made, go to *www. medalofhonor.org.*

Alexander Bonnyman Jr., born May 2, 1910, in Atlanta, Georgia

William J. Bordelon, born December 25, 1920, in San Antonio, Texas

William D. Hawkins, born April 19, 1914, in Fort Scott, Alaska

David M. Shoup, born December 30, 1904, in Tippecanoe, Indiana. Although severely shocked by an exploding enemy shell soon after landing at the pier and suffering from a serious leg wound that had become infected, Col. Shoup fearlessly exposed himself to the terrific and relentless artillery, machine guns, and rifle fire from hostile shore emplacements. Rallying his hesitant troops by his own heroism, he gallantly led them across the reefs to charge the heavily fortified island and reinforce our hard-pressed, thinly held lines. Upon arriving on shore, he assumed command of all landed troops, and working without rest and under constant withering enemy fire during the next two days, he conducted smashing attacks against unbelievably strong and fanatically defended Japanese positions despite innumerable obstacles and heavy casualties. Col. Shoup was largely responsible for the final decisive defeat of the enemy.

THE BATTLE FOR KWAJALEIN AND ROI NAMUR IN THE MARSHALL ISLANDS

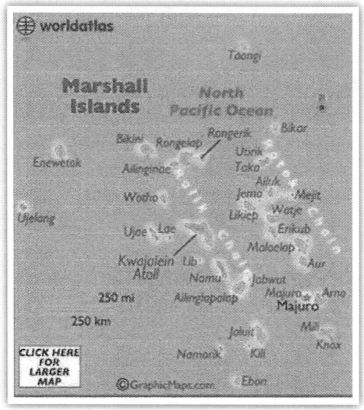

**Kwajalein Island (center of map),
steppingstone for the invasion of Saipan
(Courtesy of World atlas)**

The battle for Kwajalein and Roi Namur was fought during January and February 1944. It was the next step in the march up the ladder toward the Japanese homeland. It was significant, because it was the first time the US had attacked the so-called "outer ring" of the Japanese Pacific sphere. Also, it was the last time the Japanese tried to stop an invasion at the beaches. From that time forward, the Japanese chose a strategy of putting minimum defenses at the beach heads and concentrated on setting up bunkers and heavy gun emplacements to put the American troops in crossfire.

On January 22, 1944, the USS J. Franklin Bell sailed with the Southern Task Force for the invasion of Kwajalein Atoll. Training exercises were conducted en route, and the atoll was sighted at 0700 on January 31. A beach reconnaissance boat of volunteers was sent to the USS Monrovia, where it joined three other boats from other APAs for a mission to move within a short distance of the beach to survey the conditions of the reef and the extent of beach defenses. Battleships moved in close and covered the group with bombardment of the beaches, which demolished the beach defenses.

For the first assault wave, troops were transferred to LSTs for landing the next day with amphibious tractors. The next day, all boats were lowered, and the remaining troops were sent to the beach. The Bell moved inside the lagoon and finished unloading supplies and equipment. Casualties were received, and the Bell furnished fuel and supplies to destroyers, LSTs, and other small craft in the area.

I loved this location in the Pacific, because later in the war, when we went into the lagoon at Kwajalein, the captain allowed us to go swimming. It was a beautiful spot surrounded by coral reefs.

For the next several months, the *Bell* was busy transporting troops back and forth between the US and Honolulu and was also repaired in San Pedro, California.

Table 9: Troop casualties at Kwajalein and Roi-Namur

Kwajalein:

TROOP	USA	JAPAN
Killed	142	4,300
Wounded	845	-

Roi-Namur:

TROOP	USA	JAPAN
Killed	206	3,500
Wounded	617	-
Captured	181*	87

The following four troop members were awarded the Medal of Honor for action in the Battle for Kwajalein.

Richard B. Anderson, born June 26, 1921, in Tacoma, Washington
Aquilla James Dyess, born January 11, 1909, in Augusta, Georgia
John Vincent Power, born November 20, 1918, in Worcester, Massachusetts
Richard Keith Sorenson, born August 28, 1924, in Anoka, Minnesota

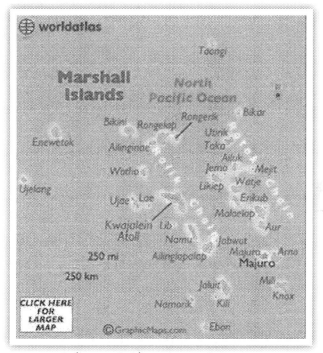

**Eniwetok (upper left) continued the preparation
for three battles in the Marianas
(Courtesy of World atlas)**

The battle for Eniwetok was fought during February 1944. It followed the battle for Kwajalein as part of the Marshall Islands campaign to secure naval and land air bases to support the battle for the next rungs in the ladder, which were Saipan, Tinian, and Guam of the Mariana Islands. The Mariana Islands were important because they brought Tokyo within range of the new B-29 bombers. The Japanese knew this, and that was the reason for their desperate attempt to intercept the invasion of Saipan, which resulted in the naval battle in the Philippine Sea.

In 1943, the Japanese had established a light defense at Eniwetok on the Islands of Engebi and Parry. The Japanese defense on Engebi was stronger than expected, so additional bombardments were brought in for the island of Parry. The result was that the regimental commander radioed at 7:30 p.m. after the landing at 9:00 a.m. on the same day, "I present you with the Island of Parry."

Table 10: Troop casualties for the battle of Eniwetok

TROOPS	USA	JAPAN
Killed	313	3,380
Wounded	879	-
Captured	77*	105

*Missing, probably from drowning

The following Medal of Honor was awarded for actions during the battle for Eniwetok.

Anthony Peter Damato, born March 28, 1922, in Shenandoah, Pennsylvania. Damato served with an assault company in action against enemy Japanese forces on Engebi Island, Eniwetok Atoll, Marshall Islands, on February 19–20, 1944. Highly vulnerable to sudden attacks by small, fanatical groups of Japanese still at large despite the efficient and determined efforts of our forces to clear the area, Cpl. Damato lay with two comrades in a large foxhole in his company's defense perimeter, which had been dangerously thinned by the forced withdrawal of nearly half of the available men. When one of the enemies approached the foxhole undetected and threw in a hand grenade, Cpl. Damato desperately groped for it in the darkness. Realizing the imminent peril to all three and fully aware of the consequences of his act, he unhesitatingly flung himself on the grenade, and although he was instantly killed as his body absorbed the explosion, he saved the lives of his two companions.

THE BATTLE OF THE PHILIPPINE SEA

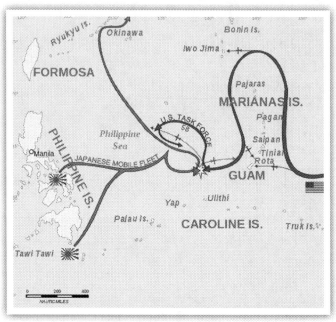

The battle of the Philippine Sea was one of the
most decisive battles in World War II because it
defeated the Japanese Navy and provided a base for
bombing the Japanese with the new B-29 bombers.
(Courtesy of Wikipedia, the free
encyclopedia—public domain)

During the battle of the Philippine Sea, in the US, celebrations
were underway with the success of the invasion of Normandy
on June 6, 1944. Prices of goods and services in the US were
modestly on the rise. Gas was priced at $0.15 per gallon; a new
home cost, on average, $3,450. The average wage had increased
to $2,400 per year; the average cost to rent a house per month
was $50. A loaf of bread cost $0.10, and sadly, Glen Miller was
reported as missing in action.

The battle of the Philippine Sea was fought in June 1944 under the leadership of Admiral Raymond Spruance and was a crushing defeat for the once proud Navy of the Japanese Empire. This battle took place about 180 miles west of Saipan and came about as result of the Japanese attempt to intercept the invasion of Saipan. The commander of the Japanese fleet was Admiral Ozawa, who launched sixty-nine planes as his first wave. The American pilots shot down forty-two of this first wave, an action that came to be known as "the Great Marianas Turkey Shoot" when one of the pilots said, "It is just like a turkey shoot back home."

Ozawa's second wave followed with 128 planes being launched, and again, they were met by the Americans with seventy more planes being shot down. Twice more, the Japanese launched more planes, and twice more, the results were the same. In total, Ozawa had put 373 planes in the air, and only 130 had returned. This number did not include about fifty land-based planes on Guam that were also shot down. The Japanese Navy air arm had lost about three-fourth of its planes. In addition to planes, the Japanese Navy had lost three fleet carriers and three oilers. Another six ships were damaged. Lt. Alexander Vraciu downed six Japanese dive bombers in one mission.

Adm. Mitscher, with Adm. Spruance's approval, set out in pursuit of the Japanese fleet. It was spotted late in the afternoon on June 20, 1944. Mitscher knew full well that his pilots might not make it back before dark, and the distance was borderline with fuel capacity of the jet planes. Sixty-five more Japanese planes were shot down, and several ships were sunk or damaged. This happened at twilight, and Adm. Mitscher, at the risk of submarine attack, turned on all carriers' lights to help the returning pilots. The result was that many did not make it back and landed in the ocean. For the US, it was a two-day loss of 130 planes and seventy-five pilots. But for the Japanese, it was defeat, as they had only about thirty-five planes left of the nearly five hundred, they started with at the beginning of battle. This defeat meant that there was no longer any hope of rescue for the Japanese on Saipan. Also, the Japanese knew that the bombing of their homeland was just a matter of time with the Marianas being an easy hop with the US's new B-29 Bombers.

Table 11: Troop, ship, and aircraft carrier casualties for the battle of the Philippine Sea

TROOP	USA	JAPAN
Killed	75	250
Wounded	100	-
Captured	-	-

SHIP/ CARRIER	USA		JAPAN	
	Destroyed	Damaged	Destroyed	Damaged
Aircraft Carrier	-	-	3	-
Aircraft (planes)	123	-	550-645	-
Oiler Ships	-	-	2	-
Other Ships	-	-	-	6
Battleship	-	1	-	-

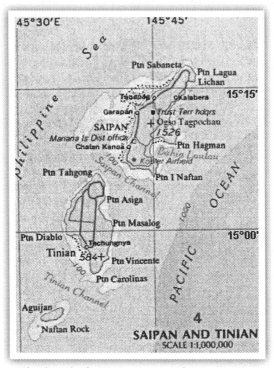

**The battle for Saipan was the crowning
blow to the Japanese military, because they
realized the homeland would be under
attack from the American B-29 bombers.
(Courtesy of US Navy public domain)**

The battle for Saipan, which was fought in June and July of
1944, has extra significance for me, because it was the first of
four battles that I experienced in the war in the Pacific. I went
aboard the USS J. Franklin Bell in February 1944 and almost
immediately went on a trip to Hawaii. I then went back to San
Pedro, California, where the ship spent the next forty-five days
in dry dock, getting repairs and alterations. I remember it well,
because I kept telling myself, I came to fight a war, and all I

am doing is spending my time on fire watch duty, observing welders make repairs. But the time passed quickly, and by May 13, 1944, the ship had moved to Honolulu and loaded army equipment and supplies. On May 18, army troops came aboard, and amphibious landings were practiced at Malaise Bay, Maui, and Kahoolawe. By that time, I had been selected to become a gunner's mate, which became my duty for the rest of my tour on the Bell.

At that point, the US had at its disposal the new long-range B-29 bomber, which could operate around a radius of 1,500 miles. The homeland of Japan was only 1,300 miles to the west. Saipan became an enormously important base for the air war on Japan. On June 15, the assault troops were landed on Saipan, along with the Bell's beach party, and the unloading of combat equipment was started.

At that same moment, it was discovered that the Japanese fleet was about 180 miles to the southwest and headed for Saipan. Adm. Spruance, Commander of the US Fifth Fleet, ordered all transports to flee to the east and await the outcome of the naval battle in the Philippine Sea. This did not allow time for the Bell to pick up the beach party or the LCVPs in action. So, we remained on the beach for more than a week, getting our supplies of food and water from what we could steal from the army and marines. I remember very well getting caught taking a carton of food off a sledge being pulled down the beach with a jeep. The carton contained food meant for officers, which was far higher in quality than the K and C rations we enlisted men had to eat. When I explained to the soldier that we had been abandoned by our ship, he felt sorry for us and asked how many were in our group. When I responded, he said, "Take another case." I made a hit with our group, because the cartons had cheese, crackers, and candy bars, among other things.

Upon landing, we were told to dig a foxhole—which we did, but not very deep. At about dusk, a Japanese plane came strafing down the beach, and we all opened fire. The sky was full of red tracer bullets, and that represented only about one-third of all bullets, because we had normally loaded every third bullet to be a tracer. We did that because the tracers became a good aiming tool. We enlarged our foxholes after that close call event. I can still hear the army men adjacent to us the next morning saying, "Did you see how fast those navy guys were expanding their foxholes after that strafing run last night?"

The invasion of Saipan completely surprised the Japanese, because they had predicted the US would attack further south. The battle for the Philippine Sea, which resulted in great losses for the Japanese Navy, made it virtually impossible for them to resupply Saipan. The island of Saipan had been under the control of the Spanish and then later the Germans before WWI. At the end of WWI, the League of Nations mandated the island of Saipan to Japanese. Therefore, a large group of Japanese civilians lived on the island—the best estimate was about 25,000. Emperor Hirohito was very disturbed by the risk that many would find the treatment by the US acceptable, and this might cause the civilians to aid the Americans in a propaganda war. Therefore, he sent out an imperial order encouraging the civilians on Saipan to commit suicide rather than surrender. They were promised an equal spiritual life in the afterlife as that of soldiers dying in combat. Thousands followed his advice.

At the northern tip of Saipan is a plateau about eight hundred feet above the rocky coral beach below. From this point, the Japanese parents threw their children off the cliff and followed them by jumping to their death on the coral below. The Japanese troops did essentially the same thing by staging one of the most furious banzai attacks of the war in the Pacific. The troops charged with guns, grenades, bayonets, and sticks and were slaughtered by the Americans—but not without heavy losses. Machine gunners had to move their weapons higher in order to shoot over the pile of Japanese bodies.

THE STORY OF WILLIAM J. O'BRIEN

Early on July 7, 1944, Lt. Colonel William J. O'Brien was killed in action during a massive attack by the desperate Japanese in a suicide attack. His last words were, "Don't give them a damned inch." The Japanese soldiers had been instructed to die for the emperor, and in dying, to take at least seven Americans soldiers with them. The Japanese tried everything to confuse the Americans, like putting women and children in front of their attacking force to give our forces the idea that they were surrendering. Also, at night, they used the ruse of having one of their soldiers run down the front line, shouting, "Shoot me! Shoot me!" hoping the marines would fire, giving away their position.

The battalion historian of O'Brien's group described the colonel as a cocky little rooster of a man who couldn't stand still.

When the tanks supporting his battalion began firing on our own troops by mistake, he was unable to make contact by radio, so he ran through enemy fire to the lead tank and pounded on the turret with his 45 pistol to get their attention and to correct the direction in which they were firing. He stayed exposed to enemy fire on top of the tank until the battle ended. He then came down off the tank and carried a wounded comrade back to the rear to get medical attention. The following is a detailed description of his citation.

> For conspicuous gallantry and intrepidity at
> the risk of his life above and beyond the call of
> duty at Saipan, Marianas Islands, from 20 June

through 7 July 1944. When assault elements of his platoon were held up by intense enemy fire, Lt. Col. O'Brien ordered three tanks to precede the assault companies in an attempt to knock out the strongpoint. Due to direct enemy fire the tanks' turrets were closed, causing the tanks to lose direction and to fire into our own troops. Lt. Col. O'Brien, with complete disregard for his own safety, dashed into full view of the enemy and ran to the leader's tank and pounded on the tank with his pistol butt to attract two of the tank's crew and, mounting the tank fully exposed to the enemy fire, Lt. Col. O'Brien personally directed the assault until the enemy strongpoint had been liquidated. On 28 June 1944, while his platoon was attempting to take a bitterly defended high ridge in the vicinity of Donnay, Lt. Col. O'Brien arranged to capture the ridge by a double envelopment movement of two large combat battalions. He personally took control of the maneuver. Lt. Col. O'Brien crossed 1,200 yards of sniper- infested underbrush alone to arrive at a point where one of his platoons was being held up by the enemy. Leaving some men to contain the enemy, he personally led four men into a narrow ravine behind and killed or drove off all the Japanese manning that strongpoint. In this action he captured five machine guns and one 77-mm fieldpiece. Lt. Col. O'Brien then organized the two platoons for night defense and against repeated counterattacks directed them. Meanwhile he managed to hold ground. On 7 July 1944 his battalion and another battalion were attacked by an overwhelming enemy force estimated at between 3,000 and 5,000 Japanese. With bloody hand-to-hand fighting in progress everywhere, their forward positions were finally overrun by the sheer weight of the enemy numbers. With many casualties and ammunition running low, Lt. Col. O'Brien refused to leave the front lines. Striding up and down the lines, he fired at the enemy with a pistol in each hand and his presence there bolstered the spirits of the men, encouraged them in their fight, and sustained them in their heroic stand. Even after he was seriously wounded, Lt. Col. O'Brien refused to be evacuated and after his pistol ammunition was exhausted, he manned a .50-caliber machine gun, mounted on a jeep, and continued firing. When last seen alive he was standing upright firing into the Jap hordes that were enveloping him. Sometime later his body was found surrounded by enemy he had killed. His valor was consistent with the highest traditions of the service.

THE STORY OF THOMAS BAKER DURING THE BATTLE FOR SAIPAN

Sergeant Thomas Baker is an example of the fight put up by the Americans. He was seriously wounded, and when his unit withdrew to a better defensive position, the medic helping him was also wounded. Baker said, "Look, I am not going to make it. Just prop me up by that tree and give me a pistol and a cigarette." The pistol had eight rounds of ammunition. The next morning, as his unit moved forward, he was found dead, the cigarette butt clinging to his lips but eight Japanese bodies lying around him. For his heroic action, he received the Medal of Honor. The complete citation reads as follows.

> For conspicuous gallantry and intrepidity at the risk of his life above and beyond the call of duty at Saipan, Mariana Islands, 19 June to 7 July 1944. When his entire company was held up by fire from automatic weapons and small-arms fire from strongly fortified enemy positions that commanded the view of the company, Sgt. (then Pvt.) Baker voluntarily took a bazooka and dashed alone to within 100 yards of the enemy. Through heavy rifle and machinegun fire that was directed at him by the enemy, he knocked out the strong point, enabling his company to assault the ridge. Some days later while his company advanced across the open field flanked with obstructions and places of concealment for the enemy, Sgt. Baker again voluntarily took up

a position in the rear to protect the company against surprise attack and came upon 2 heavily fortified enemy pockets manned by 2 officers and 10 enlisted men which had been bypassed. Without regard for such superior numbers, he unhesitatingly attacked and killed all of them. Five hundred yards farther, he discovered 6 men of the enemy who had concealed themselves behind our lines and destroyed all of them. On 7 July 1944, the perimeter of which Sgt. Baker was a part was attacked from 3 sides by from 3,000 to 5,000 Japanese. During the early stages of this attack, Sgt. Baker was seriously wounded but he insisted on remaining in the line and fired at the enemy at ranges sometimes as close as 5 yards until his ammunition ran out. Without ammunition and with his own weapon battered to uselessness from hand-to-hand combat, he was carried about 50 yards to the rear by a comrade, who was then himself wounded. At this point Sgt. Baker refused to be moved any farther stating that he preferred to be left to die rather than risk the lives of any more of his friends. A short time later, at his request, he was placed in a sitting position against a small tree. Another comrade, withdrawing, offered assistance. Sgt. Baker refused, insisting that he be left alone and be given a soldier's pistol with its remaining 8 rounds of ammunition. When last seen alive, Sgt. Baker was propped against a tree, pistol in hand, calmly facing the foe. Later Sgt. Baker's body was found in the same position, gun empty, with 8 Japanese lying dead before him.

A couple days later, as the fighting ended, 4,311 Japanese bodies were counted on the beach at Tanapag. The Japanese General Saito, when all appeared lost, sat down in his cave headquarters, had a dinner of canned crabmeat and sake, and then committed suicide. Admiral Nagumo, the naval commander for Saipan, also committed suicide.

The Bell returned to the area on June 25 and finished unloading equipment and supplies. She then sailed for Eniwetok on June 16, where the ship was replenished with fuel and supplies. We of the beach party were transferred to the USS Cavalier and sent back to Saipan, where we made plans for the invasion of Tinian.

It was on the Cavalier that we met the Hollywood actor Caesar Romero. He was a part of that crew. It seemed strange to see him hosing down decks like an enlisted man. But it did not seem to bother him. A few months later, someone posted a newspaper article on our ship's bulletin board showing Caesar with his arms around Betty Gable and a caption saying, "He was glad to get home to see his mother."

As previously noted, Janice and I visited Saipan in December 2017. The following is our story.

THE RETURN VISIT TO SAIPAN AND TINIAN IN DECEMBER 2017

I searched unsuccessfully for years to find a cruise that would take me and my wife back to some of the Islands where I fought on during WWII. Then one day, an ad appeared on my website from Beyond Band of Brothers Tour Group for a tour of Guam, Saipan, Tinian, and Okinawa. I contacted them; sent a copy of my book, *Forgotten Warriors;* and offered to be a host for this trip. I was told that I should stop by their office in Lexington, Kentucky, to discuss the tour. During the visit, I was told they already had local guides on each Island to host the tour, but since I was a WWII veteran, my trip would be free except for airfare to Guam and back. They also gave my wife a 25 percent discount. We left for Guam on December 8, 2017, and returned to Dayton, Ohio on December 24, 2017.

During this trip, I was exposed to a fact that had never crossed my mind. We not only fought to keep Americans free, but also to free a lot of natives on the islands who had been under Japanese control for many years. Such is the case of the Chamorros of the Marianas Islands (Guam, Saipan, Tinian, etc.). These islands were discovered by the Spanish explorer Ferdinand Magellan in 1521 during his first voyage around the world. Then, in the 1600s, the Queen of Spain, Maria Anna, sent missionaries to these islands. From this effort by the Queen of Spain came the name *Marianas.*

The Chamorros were the original native group, and in all probability, they migrated from the nearby Caroline Islands.

When WWII started, there were about 3,900 natives on the islands of Saipan and Tinian. (Tinian is situated about four miles south of Saipan.)

We visited the American Memorial Park where the names of more than five thousand who were killed are engraved in marble. Our tour guide told us not to worry if we did not see everything that day, because we were returning the next day to observe a ceremony. He gave no clue as to the purpose of the ceremony.

The next day, as promised, we returned to the park. The park officials asked me to step forward. They then read the following.

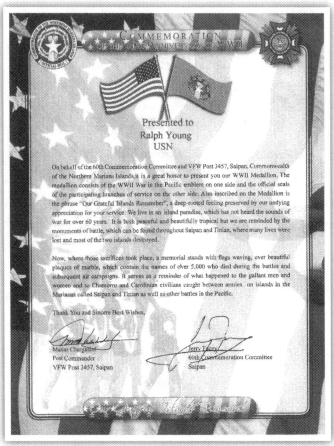

Proclamation by the Chamorros of the VFW 3457
(Courtesy of D. Ralph Young, public domain)

The park officials had discovered that I was with the D-day invasions of both Saipan and Tinian and made the award on behalf of local people with the words, "Our grateful islands remember." This was the highlight of our tour. I am just disappointed that it took all these years for me to finally realize that other people were enslaved by the Japanese and that our actions set them free.

During the rest of our time on Saipan and Tinian, whether in restaurants or on the beach, I was greeted with handshakes, hugs, and photographs. It was a thrill of a lifetime. I told them at the ceremony that I was coming again next year. But on second thought, at ninety-four years of age, I guess I will have to pass.

We visited an area where the Japanese had directed the locals to congregate during our invasion. There was no housing, just an open area with a creek flowing through. The Chamorros said that they lived off the land, as many different fruits were available. They also said that they were not confronted with guards keeping them in the area, because there was just no place to go. They lived in this area until the invasion was over. When visiting the beach with some of the local people, one gentleman told me proudly how his father had joined the Americans on D-day. He also revealed that he was one of his father's twenty-two children. I inquired as to the size of his family, and he answered, "Five." He then explained that the difference in family size was the result of television.

The following is a copy of a letter to the editor of a local Kentucky newspaper I wrote describing our trip to the Marianas.

> Tomorrow we leave Guam for Saipan. The past week we have spent time in Tokyo and Guam. Tokyo is impressive with a beautiful skyline in all directions. I have been there several times and always marvel how clean they keep the city. But, to be honest, I never fail to have this uncomfortable feeling when I see Japanese my

age as I wonder if they are the ones that fought like "Barbarians" during WWII. I guess I feel like the native Chamorros who live here on Guam. We observed the area where they were detained in the middle of the jungle and survived by living off the land of fruits and vegetables. Also, we saw how terrible the Chamorros were treated by the Japanese after Guam was occupied the day after Pearl Harbor. I read today a quote by the Chamorros which said they were willing to forgive BUT, they will never forget.

This is how a Japanese soldier lived on Guam for twenty-seven years after the war.
(Courtesy of D. Ralph Young, public domain)

The above illustration shows how a Japanese soldier survived here on Guam for twenty-seven years after the war ended before he surrendered. I saw the actual sight today in the middle of the jungle.

The following is an article I agreed to write for our local newspaper to describe my feelings after being away for seventy-three years.

I was the only one in the tour group involved in combat during WWII. There were many questions from our tour members. Tomorrow we leave for Saipan. I do not know at this point what my feelings and reaction will be when I see the same beaches again where I landed as an 18-year-old kid. Of course, being 18 and from Lincoln County, Kentucky, I thought then I could conquer the world. The truth is I had no idea how big the world was at that time in my life.

My reaction as we circled to land at the airport was a surprise - seeing so many high-rise buildings and beautiful white sandy beaches. This time the bodies lying on the beach were sun bathers rather than dead bodies. I had difficulty pinpointing the exact spot but, when I described two features that I remember from 73 years ago, our guide said this is the spot.

Our guide was a well-educated American who came to Saipan many years ago. He is married to a native Chamorro (the name of the indigenous tribe) and has served in the Local government since it was established after WWII. The entire tour group insisted that he and I pose for pictures on the spot where I had landed on June 15, 1944 the rest of the day was spent visiting battle sites throughout the southern part of the Island and the American Memorial Park. The guide said if you do not see everything in the Park today, you will get second chance tomorrow, as we are coming back for a ceremony.

The following day we spent all morning in the Northern part of the Island. We visited Suicide Cliff and Banzai Cliff, where thousands jumped to their death because the brain washing had convinced the civilians that the Americans were cruel and barbarian people.

Award ceremony with park official
who made the award
(Courtesy of Janice Young, public domain)

After lunch, we came back to the American Memorial Park for the surprise of my life. The National Park Service for the Marianas Islands was there to award me a medal for "WWII Valor in the Pacific."

They just do not get many WWII veterans visiting anymore. I have been one of the lucky ones too, as I am still blessed with reasonably good health and strength. If you have read my book *The Power of a Mother's Prayer* you know the answer as to why I have good health.

Flying from Saipan to Tinian
(Photo by D. Ralph Young, public domain)

The next day, we traveled to the island of Tinian on small piper cub planes. The trip took fewer than ten minutes, but the only way to get there was by plane, as the ferry service stopped a couple of years ago. Here is a picture of Janice and me aboard the small plane.

This time, it was not too difficult to find where I landed, because White Beach One was such a small beach. During WWII, I was with a group that had been transferred to the ship APA 37 (USS Caviler), because my ship was to be a part of the fake landing on the southern beaches, and we had to go in with assault troops. We swam the last hundred yards into the beach with a floating pier that would allow us to bridge over the coral reefs to land troops, equipment, and supplies. The fake landings worked, and we had very little resistance from the Japanese. Also, Tinian is very flat and open, so the Japanese could not move their troops north to oppose the landing, because the ships offshore kept them pinned down. Admiral Spruance called this the most brilliant amphibious operation of WWII. I am proud to have been a part of the operation.

Next, we went on to Okinawa. This means we got up at 1:30 a.m. to fly to Guam; then, we went on to Fukuoka, Japan, before changing planes for Okinawa. Our tour guide Camille and a new friend Russ made the trip easy with their youth and energy.

Our first day on Okinawa was spent seeing the beaches where our troops met the Japanese. We also visited the many caves that both the Japanese and the people of Okinawa used for hiding during the battle. I was able to observe the vast bay where my comrade and I generated smoke to hide our ships from the Japanese, especially the kamikaze planes that sunk so many of our ships during the battle for Okinawa.

I will send the next report in a few days.

D. Ralph Young
12-19-2017

Table 12: Troop casualties that occurred at Saipan

TROOP	USA	JAPAN
Killed	3,426	24,000*
Wounded	10,364	-
Captured	-	921**

* Additional 5,000 Japanese suicides

**Additional 22,000 Japanese civilians dead (mostly suicides)

The following seven troop members were awarded the Medal of Honor for their action during the battle for Saipan. The story for O'Brian and Baker are included. For additional stories, go to *www.themedalofhonor.org*.

Harold Christ Agerholm, born January 25,1925 in Racine, Wisconsin

Thomas A. Baker, born June 25, 1916, in Troy, New York

Harold G. Epperson, born June 25, 1923, in Akron, Ohio

Robert H. McCard, born November 25, 1918, in Syracuse, New York

William O'Brien, date of birth not recorded, born in Troy, New York

Ben L. Salomon, born September 1, 1914, in Milwaukee, Wisconsin

Grant Frederick Timmerman, born February 14, 1919, in Americus, Kansas

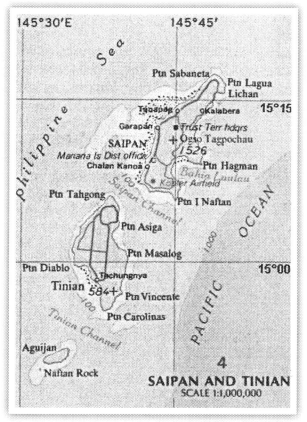

145°30'E   145°45'

Sea

Ptn Sabaneta
Ptn Lagua
Lichan
15°15
Tapapag   Kalabera
Garapan   Trust Terr hdqrs
SAIPAN   Ogso Tagpochau
1526
Mariana Is Dist office
Chalan Kanoa   Ptn Hagman
Bahia Laulau
Koller Airfield
Ptn Tahgong   Ptn I Naftan
OCEAN
Ptn Asiga
1000
Ptn Masalog
Ptn Diablo   15°00
Tinian   Tchungnya
584   Ptn Vincente
PACIFIC
Ptn Carolinas
Aguijan
4
Naftan Rock   SAIPAN AND TINIAN
SCALE 1:1,000,000

Philippine

Saipan Channel

Tinian Channel

**The battle for Saipan was the crowning blow to
the Japanese military because they realized
The homeland would be under attack
from the American B-29 bombers
(Courtesy of US Navy public domain)**

In the course of the battle, the nine thousand-man Japanese garrison was eliminated. The island, along with Saipan and Guam, became the base for the twentieth air force. It was from this island that the atomic bombs were loaded for the trip to Hiroshima and Nagasaki. Due to the flat terrain, Tinian was better suited for the B-29 airstrips than Saipan. Fifteen thousand seabees turned the island into the busiest airfield of the war.

The invasion of Tinian was difficult, because the only desirable beach for landing was on the south of the island. Everyone knew that the Japanese would have this area heavily fortified. There was a slight opening on the northwest side of the island, but it was small. The decision was made to fake an invasion to the south beaches to draw the defenders in that direction and then land on the small beach in the north. The Bell and other transports got underway and proceeded to the southern tip of the island. Boats were lowered, and the embarkation was simulated. The boat waves were formed and sent toward the beaches. When they got to within 1,500 yards, the Japanese shore batteries opened fire with a heavy barrage, but none of the LCVPs was hit. However, the ships Colorado and Norman Scott were hit and suffered heavy casualties. The boats retreated to a safe area and regrouped.

The boat waves were reformed and sent toward the beach a second time. This time, they turned off at five thousand yards, and no fire was received from the beach.

In the meantime, the Bell boat group commander, beach party, and boat crews played a major role in the actual amphibious strike on the northern beaches. As we approached the beach, we did not know if the fake landings worked to draw the Japanese troops to the south of the island. The closer we got to the beach, the better we felt, because the gunfire from the beach was extremely light. The fact that Tinian was very flat and narrow enabled our warships offshore to keep the troops who went south pinned down so they could not get back to the north, where we were landing. I remember that we managed to get a floating dock that was long enough to reach just beyond the coral reef, where we brought vehicles and troops onto the shore. I also remember the occasional jeep that failed to hit the ramp and ended up being submerged in about ten feet of water. I thought to myself, *How I would like to have one of them back on the farm in Kentucky.*

After hoisting the LCVPs back aboard, the Bell and other APAs proceeded to the north of the island, where the actual landing was taking place. Assault troops were landed, and casualties were brought back to our ship. It was during this landing that our boats came under heavy fire by Japanese field guns and mortars, and William Kalnitsky in Bell boat twenty-two was wounded. On July 27, all the casualties were transferred to the field hospital on Saipan, and 438 Japanese prisoners of war were brought aboard for transfer back to Pearl Harbor.

This happens to be one of my close calls at being a casualty, because we found a young Japanese soldier hiding in a bamboo thicket. He had spent all his ammunition but attempted to use his bayonet; however, machetes and numbers won out. I kept asking myself, *didn't you join the navy to avoid this hand-to-hand combat?* I was impressed with the fact that he was nearly six feet tall and very athletically built. He suffered machete wounds during the struggle and was given a blood transfusion by a corpsman, which did not go over well with a lot of our nearby troops.

It was on Tinian that I missed seeing my nephew Earl Hutchison. He had been a part of the Tarawa invasion and had been wounded in the head. He was now fully recovered and was a part of the second marine landing on Tinian. He knew my ship number was APA-16, so he contacted the crew of one of our LCVPs and wrote me a note on the inside wrapper of a pack of Camel cigarettes, saying, "Sorry I missed seeing you, but see you back in Kentucky." And that he did.

Earl was among the group of marines who was unloaded at the reef and had to walk to the beach at Tarawa through water over his head at times plus a hail of bullets being fired by the Japanese troops. Two of every three marines in the landing were killed.

The invasion of Tinian was the US's most perfectly executed amphibious invasion; yet it has received relatively limited attention. According to reports, Admiral Raymond A. Spruance said that the seizure of Tinian was the most brilliantly conceived and executed amphibious operation in World War II.

Several years ago, my shipmate Ralph McCormack sent me an email that really caught my attention. It was so beautifully written and so accurately penned that I just had to include in my book. It follows below with permission of the author as well as a listing of her website.

Although we are blessed with a memory that helps us recall major events that happen in our lives, these memories cannot be downloaded to family or friends should the Lord say it is time to come home. That is why the written word is so meaningful and important and why this email I received fantastically brought back memories of D-day on July 24, 1944. This was the invasion of Tinian in the Marianna Island group. It was written by a lady who spent her early years in a Japanese camp. You can read about her life in *Rising from the Shadow of the Sun*. I think that most readers are appreciative when the writer has lived through his or her story.

It is sad to think, but I might be one the few remaining WWII veterans who can remember and write about WWII. This article, called "Runway Able," was written by Ronny Herman de Jong. It is about the island of Tinian and its impact on finishing WWII. The article also predicts very realistically what would have happened if we had to invade Japan. As mentioned, I was there when the fake landing on the most desirable invasion beach on the south drew the Japanese in that direction and we landed on a less desirable beach on the northwest side of Tinian. This beach is only a few hundred feet from where Runway Able was to be built.

THE STORY OF RUNWAY ABLE BY RONNY HERMAN DEJONG

TINIAN ISLAND – Runway Able – incredible Piece of WWII history
Tinian Island, Pacific Ocean.

It's a small island, less than 40 square miles, a flat green dot in the vastness of Pacific blue. Fly over it and you notice a slash across its north end of uninhabited bush, a long thin line that looks like an overgrown dirt runway. If you didn't know what it was, you wouldn't give it a second glance out your airplane window.

On the ground, you see the runway isn't dirt but tarmac and crushed limestone, abandoned with weeds sticking out of it. Yet this is arguably the most historical airstrip on earth. This is where World War II was won. This is Runway Able:

On July 24, 1944, 30,000 US Marines landed on the beaches of Tinian ... Eight days later, over 8,000 of the 8,800 Japanese soldiers on the island were dead (vs. 328 Marines), and four months later the Seabees had built the busiest airfield of WWII - dubbed North Field - enabling B-29 Super fortresses to launch air attacks on the Philippines, Okinawa, and mainland Japan.

Late in the afternoon of August 5, 1945, a B-29 was maneuvered over a bomb loading pit, then after lengthy preparations, taxied to the east end of North Field's main runway, Runway Able, and at 2:45am in the early morning darkness of August 6, took off.

The B-29 was piloted by Col. Paul Tibbets of the US Army Air Force, who had named the plane after his mother, *Enola Gay*. The crew named the bomb they were carrying *Little Boy*. 6½ hours later at 8:15am Japan time, the first atomic bomb was dropped on Hiroshima.

Three days later, in the pre-dawn hours of August 9, a B-29 named *Bockscar* (a pun on "boxcar" after its flight commander Capt. Fred Bock), piloted by Major Charles Sweeney took off from Runway Able. Finding its primary target of Kokura obscured by clouds, Sweeney proceeded to the secondary target of Nagasaki, over which, at 11:01am, bombardier Kermit Beahan released the atomic bomb dubbed *Fat Man*.

Here is Atomic Bomb Pit #1" where *Little Boy* was loaded onto *Enola Gay*:

There are pictures displayed in the pit, now glass enclosed.

This one shows *Little Boy* being hoisted into *Enola Gay*'s bomb bay.

And here on the other side of the ramp is "Atomic Bomb Pit #2" where *Fat Man* was loaded onto *Bockscar*.

The commemorative plaque records that 16 hours after the nuking of Nagasaki, "On August 10, 1945 at 0300, the Japanese Emperor without his cabinet's consent decided to end the Pacific War."

Take a good look at these pictures, folks. This is where World War II ended with total victory of America over Japan. I was there all alone. There were no other visitors, and no one lives anywhere near for miles. Visiting the Bomb Pits, walking along deserted Runway Able in solitude, was a moment of extraordinarily powerful solemnity.

It was a moment of deep reflection. Most people, when they think of Hiroshima and Nagasaki, reflect on the numbers of lives killed in the nuclear blasts - at least 70,000 and 50,000 respectively. Being here caused me to reflect on the number of lives *saved* - how many more Japanese and Americans would have died in a continuation of the war had the nukes not been dropped.

Yet that was not all. It's not just that the nukes obviated the US invasion of Japan, Operation Downfall, that would have caused upwards of a million American and Japanese deaths or more. It's that *nuking Hiroshima and Nagasaki were of extraordinary humanitarian benefit to the nation and people of Japan.*

Let's go to this cliff on the nearby island of Saipan to learn why:

Saipan is less than a mile north of Tinian ... The month before the Marines took Tinian, on June 15, 1944, 71,000 Marines landed on Saipan ... They faced 31,000 Japanese soldiers determined not to surrender.

Japan had colonized Saipan after World War I and turned the island into a giant sugar cane plantation. By the time of the Marine invasion, in addition to the 31,000 entrenched soldiers, some 25,000 Japanese settlers were living on Saipan, plus thousands more Okinawans, Koreans, and native islanders brutalized as slaves to cut the sugar cane.

There were also one or two thousand Korean "comfort women" (*kanji* in Japanese), abducted young women from Japan's colony of Korea to service the Japanese soldiers as sex slaves. (See *The Comfort Women: Japan's Brutal Regime of*

Enforced Prostitution in the Second World War, by George Hicks.)

Within a week of their landing, the Marines set up a civilian prisoner encampment that quickly attracted a couple thousand Japanese and others wanting US food and protection. When word of this reached Emperor Hirohito - who contrary to the myth was in full charge of the war - he became alarmed that radio interviews of the well-treated prisoners broadcast to Japan would subvert his people's will to fight.

As meticulously documented by historian Herbert Bix in *Hirohito and the Making of Modern Japan*, the Emperor issued an order for all Japanese civilians on Saipan to commit suicide. The order included the promise that, although the civilians were of low caste, their suicide would grant them a status in heaven equal to those honored soldiers who died in combat for their Emperor.

And that is why the precipice in the picture above is known as Suicide Cliff, off which over 20,000 Japanese civilians jumped to their deaths to comply with their fascist emperor's desire - mothers flinging their babies off the cliff first or in their arms as they jumped.

Anyone reluctant or refused, such as the Okinawan or Korean slaves, were shoved off at gunpoint by the Jap soldiers. Then the soldiers themselves proceeded to hurl themselves into the ocean to drown off a sea cliff afterwards called Banzai Cliff. Of the 31,000 Japanese soldiers on Saipan, the Marines killed 25,000, 5,000 jumped off Banzai Cliff, and only the remaining thousand were taken prisoner.

The extent of this demented fanaticism is very hard for any civilized mind to fathom - especially when it is devoted not to anything noble but barbarian evil instead. The vast brutalities inflicted by the Japanese on their conquered and colonized peoples of China, Korea, the Philippines and throughout their "Greater East Asia Co-Prosperity Sphere" was a hideously depraved horror.

And they were willing to fight to the death to defend it. So, they had to be nuked. The only way to put an end to the Japanese barbarian horror was unimaginably colossal destruction against which they had no defense whatever. Nuking Japan was not a matter of justice, revenge, or it is getting what it deserved. It was the only way to end the Japanese dementia.

And it worked - for the Japanese. They stopped being barbarians and started being civilized. They achieved more prosperity - and peace - than they ever knew or could have achieved had they continued fighting and not been nuked. The *shock* of getting nuked is responsible.

We achieved this because we were determined to achieve *victory*. Victory without apologies. Despite perennial liberal demands we do so, America and its government has never apologized for nuking Japan. Hopefully, America never will.

Oh, yes ... *Guinness* lists Saipan as having the best, most equitable, weather in the world. And the beaches? Well, take a look:

By Ronny Herman de Jong
Reprinted with permission
http://www.ronnyhermandejong.com

Here's what the beaches of Saipan looked like when I was there again in December 2017. Saipan is indeed a beautiful resort island.

D Ralph Young on Saipan in December 2017

Soldiers on the Saipan beach in June 1944
This photo (author unknown) is
licensed under CC BY-SA-NC.

Table 13: Troop casualties that occurred at Tinian

	USA	JAPAN
Killed	326	5,542
Wounded	1,593	-
Captured	-	252*

*An additional 2,265 Japanese missing

The following men were awarded the Medal of Honor for their actions during the battle for Tinian.

Joseph William Ozbourn As a BAR (Browning Automatic Rifleman) during the battle for enemy Japanese-held Tinian Island, Marianas Islands, July 30, 1944, and as a member of a platoon assigned the mission of clearing the remaining Japanese troops from dugouts and pillboxes along a tree line, Pvt. Ozbourn, flanked by two men on either side, was moving forward to throw an armed hand grenade into a dugout when a terrific blast from the entrance severely wounded the four men and himself. Unable to throw the grenade into the dugout and with no place to hurl it without endangering the other men, Pvt. Ozbourn unhesitatingly grasped it close to his body and fell upon it, sacrificing his own life to absorb the full impact of the explosion but saving his comrades.

Robert L. Wilson During action against enemy Japanese forces at Tinian Island, Marianas Group, on August 4, 1944, as one of a group of marines advancing through heavy underbrush to neutralize isolated points of resistance, Pfc. Wilson daringly preceded his companions. Serving with the 2nd Marine Division (Reinforced), Wilson received a second Presidential Unit Citation signed by Secretary of the Navy James Forrestal "for outstanding performance of duty in combat during the seizure and occupation of the Japanese held Atoll of Tarawa, Gilbert Islands, November 20, 24, 1943." In addition, Wilson received the Purple Heart with one gold star.

At the time of his death, Wilson was serving with Company D, 2nd Pioneer Battalion, 18th Marines, and the 2nd Marine Division. The Medal of Honor was presented to his mother at a ceremony held on July 26, 1945, at the American Legion cottage in Centralia. Private First-Class Wilson was initially buried in the military cemetery on Tinian but was reinterred in Hillcrest Cemetery, Centralia, Illinois, in 1948.

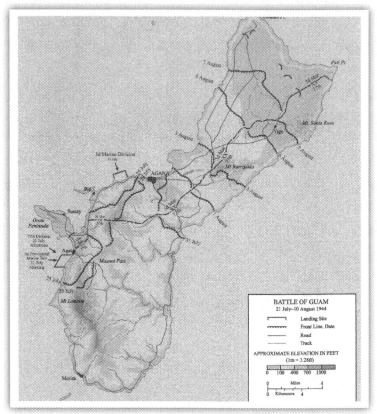

The island of Guam, largest in the Mariana group
(Courtesy of Wikimedia Commons,
the free media repository)

Guam is the largest of the Marianas islands. The island had belonged to Spain but was taken over by the US in 1898. Japan had invaded the island on December 10, 1941, three days after Pearl Harbor. Saipan, Tinian, and Guam were desirable locations for the continued move toward the Japanese mainland and for upcoming invasions of the Philippines (Leyte) and Ryukyu Islands (Okinawa). Originally, the invasion of Guam was set for three days after the invasion of Saipan. But, due the unexpected strength of the Japanese on Saipan and the Philippine Sea naval battle, it was decided to delay the attack on Guam for a month. Guam, which is ringed with cliffs and reefs and a heavy surf, was a challenge to any attacker. The Japanese were effective with their artillery, which sank twenty LVTs and inflicted heavy loss on the US troops. However, by nightfall on the first day, the Americans had a beachhead nearly seven thousand feet deep. Each counterattack by the Japanese during the night resulted in heavy losses for the enemy.

The Japanese chose to withdraw to the mountainous region in the central and northern part of the island to hold the island if possible. Rain and thick jungle made things difficult for the US troops. By August 10, 1944, organized Japanese resistance had essentially ended, and it was estimated that about 7,500 were at large in the jungle. The commander for the Japanese then committed ritual suicide at his headquarters. A few Japanese continued to hide out in the jungle, and nearly a year later, three marines were ambushed and killed. On January 24, 1972, Sergeant Shoichi Yokoi was found by hunters. He had lived alone in a cave for twenty-seven years.

Table 14: Troop casualties for the second battle for Guam

	USA	JAPAN
Killed	1,783	18,337*
Wounded	6,010	-
Captured	-	1,250

The first battle occurred on December 10, 1941, just after Pearl Harbor, when Japanese invaded the US Island.

The following four troop members were awarded the Medal of Honor for their actions during the battle for Guam. (For details on others who received the award, go to _www.themedalofhonor.org_.)

Leonard F. Mason, born February 2, 1920, in Middleborough, Kentucky. In action against the enemy on the island of Guam, suddenly taken under fire by two enemy machine guns that were holding up the advance of his platoon through a narrow gulley, Pfc. Mason, on his own initiative, climbed out of the gully and moved parallel toward the enemy position. Although wounded, he (with complete disregard to his own safety) cleaned out an enemy position, killing five enemy soldiers and wounding another. He then rejoined his platoon and reported his action before succumbing to his critical wounds. His exceptionally heroic act in the face of almost certain death enabled his platoon to accomplish its mission.

Luther Skaggs Jr., born March 3, 1923, in Henderson, Kentucky. When the section leader became a casualty under heavy mortar barrage shortly after landing, Pfc. Skaggs promptly assumed command and led his section through intense fire for a distance of two hundred yards to a position from which to deliver effective coverage of the assault on a strategic cliff. Pfc. Skaggs was critically wounded when a grenade was tossed into his foxhole. He put a tourniquet on his leg and continued gallantly to return enemy fire with his rifle and grenades for a period of eight hours. Uncomplaining and calm throughout this critical period, Pfc. Skaggs served as a heroic example of courage and fortitude to other wounded men.

Louis H. Wilson Jr., born February 11, 1920, in Brandon, Michigan
Frank P. Witek, born December 1921 in Derby, Connecticut

THE BATTLE FOR LEYTE IN THE PHILIPPINES

I shall return.

—General Douglas MacArthur, Supreme
Allied Commander of South-West Pacific
(speaking about the Philippines when he
was forced to retreat to Australia 1942)

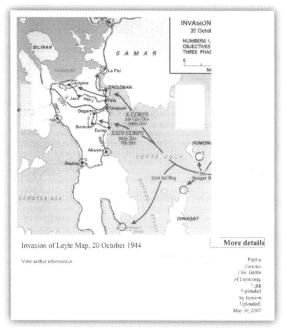

Invasion of Leyte Map, 20 October 1944

View author information

Public Domain
File: Battle of Leyte map 1.jpg Uploaded by Iraxisu Uploaded: May 30, 2007

The above map of Leyte shows MacArthur l
living up to his promise: "I shall return."
(Courtesy of Wikimedia Commons,
the free media repository)

After the battle for Tinian, the USS J. Franklin Bell returned to Pearl Harbor, where we unloaded the prisoners of war and took on US troops and combat equipment. Amphibious practice landings were held at Maalaen Bay on the island of Maui for several days. After this, the troops were returned to their land base. During the next two weeks, final planning for the invasion of Yap Island was completed. Our first stop was at Eniwetok in the Marshall Islands. The general in charge of the troops aboard left the ship for a meeting, returning to announce that a new objective: Leyte in the Philippines. The Bell then headed for Manus in the Admiralty Islands Group. Anti-aircraft practice was held every day while in route to Manus.

One of the sections of the barrier reef north of the harbor, Pityliu Island, was set aside for rest and relaxation. I became very popular with the "old salts" on board, because at my young age, I was not yet a beer drinker, and we were restricted to just a couple beers for each shipmate. I quite frequently traded my beers for Cokes.

For the assault on Leyte, the Bell assistant beach master (with some of the beach party members) was transferred to the LST 605. Other APAs did the same for another five LSTs. They were accompanied by 926 assault troops. The goal for this advanced group was to hit the beach to test the Japanese defense for the landing that was to follow.

The task group moved out of Seeadler Harbor, where firing exercises were a daily routine. *Mindanao* was detected by radar late on October 19, 1944. During the night, the convoy sailed through Surigao Straits and entered Leyte Gulf. At dawn, Japanese planes flew over the convoy just a few hundred feet above, dropping bombs that landed on each side of the Bell but did not inflict any damage. I can still, to this day, see visions of the plane directly overhead through a gap in the smoke screen.

Directly behind the beach was a small ridge about three hundred to four hundred feet above sea level. The Japanese planes used the ridge to hide from our radar and would pop over the hill and be upon us without any warning. On one occasion, an American plane was chasing a Japanese plane that was flying in over the ridge. The Japanese plane was shot down as well as our own plane. The American pilot was rescued from the gulf by one of our LCVPs and brought aboard our ship. He was very angry and said all he would do if he could find out who shot him down. All my shipmates said it was not us. But since I was captain of the aft 40 mm gun crew and was firing our guns with all the rest of the ships in the area, I could not rule us out as being the guilty party, especially since he said a round of ammunition went right between his legs, which he suspected to be a 40 mm projectile.

The landing was executed with great precision, and the Bell immediately started to receive casualties for treatment by returning landing craft. At midafternoon, the cruiser Honolulu (just north of the Bell) was torpedoed by an enemy plane. At about dusk, several Japanese planes flew over our anchorage without inflicting any damage. The smoke screen was so thick that we could not fire our guns, and the Japanese planes could not bomb or execute a kamikaze. However, at dawn the next morning, the cruiser Australia was hit by a kamikaze. Minutes later, two Japanese planes came diving out of the sun, but fortunately for us, they chose other targets. l will never forget looking down from our aft 40mm gun turret into the conning tower of LSM-34 that pulled alongside our ship for help and seeing the mangled bodies of three comrades. A mortar shell had pierced the command post. Another thing I remember vividly is the thickness of the smoke from damaged ships, bombing, gunfire, and smoke screens we created to hide from the kamikaze planes. How we were able to maneuver blindly through the Leyte Gulf full of ships without colliding remains a mystery to me.

THE NAVAL BATTLE OF LEYTE GULF

The naval battle of Leyte Gulf had some first and last components. It was the first time the Japanese used the kamikaze plane as a defensive weapon; it was also the last time in history for battleship-to-battleship combat. The Americans had the advantage in the battleship combat because of advanced developments in radar technology. Our range and accuracy were much better than those of the Japanese.

The IJN mobilized nearly all their remaining fleet in a desperate attempt to stop the invasion of the Philippines. I shudder when I think how close we of the invasion force came to annihilation in the invasion of the island of Leyte. Admiral Halsey has received many glowing reports about his action during WWII, which he earned. He was greatly admired by the enlisted men who served under him. However, his short fuse and quick temper nearly created a disaster in the naval battle of Leyte Gulf. This engagement consisted of several battles, such as Sibuyan Sea, Surigao Strait, Cape Engano, and the battle off Samar. Had it not been for the heroic action of a few destroyers and escort carriers, the invasion of Leyte would have had a different conclusion.

The IJN had divided its ships into three fleets: the northern, the center, and the southern. The plan was to use the northern fleet as bait to lure Halsey 3rd fleet away from the entrance to Leyte Gulf. This northern fleet would have several aircraft carriers but few planes and pilots, because with Halsey raids on the Islands of Formosa and the Ryukyu and Admiral

Spruance's success in the previous battle of the Philippine Sea (the Marianna's Turkey shoot), the Japanese air force was nearly destroyed. As the 3rd fleet was being led away from Leyte Gulf, the southern and center forces would attack the US invasion force from the west and north. The center force was by far the most powerful, as it consisted of five battleships, ten heavy cruisers, two light cruisers, and fifteen destroyers.

Now, an image comes to my mind of my early childhood. I loved watching western movies and seeing the Lone Ranger coming to the rescue. Enter the submarine force—the one with the greatest percentage of loss of life of any WWII force. The Darter and Dace detected the Japanese formation some six miles away. They traveled at full speed to get into position to make an attack at sunrise. The attack was very successful. However, Darter ran aground, and all efforts to free her failed. Her crew was transferred to the Dace. The Nautilus arrived on the scene, and with her six-inch guns, she made sure the Darter was only good for scrap.

The 3rd Fleet was not in a good position to deal with the Japanese threat to Leyte Gulf. Some of its ships had been sent to Ulithi to take on provisions and rearm. The delay in getting these ships back deprived the 3rd Fleet of about 40 percent of its air strength. The 3rd Fleet had failed to locate the northern force they were searching for, mainly because they were preoccupied with air attacks from the center force. This meant that the only Japanese force that wanted to be found was the one that could not be found. Halsey was convinced that the northern force was the main Japanese threat. He was determined to seize what he thought was a great opportunity to destroy the last remaining carrier strength of the IJN. Halsey and his staff ignored information about the threat to Leyte Gulf on two occasions. The staff on Admiral Mitscher's ship became worried to the point that they decided to awaken Mitscher with concerns about the situation. His response was, "Does Admiral Halsey have the report?" When told yes, he said, "If Halsey wants my advice, he will ask," and he went back to sleep. The entire strength of the 3rd Fleet continued to steam northward, leaving the San Bernardino Strait and Leyte Gulf completely unguarded.

Halsey defended his decision in a dispatch after the battle by saying,

> Searches by my carrier planes revealed the presence of the Northern carrier force which completed the picture of all enemy naval forces. As it seemed childish to me to guard statically San Bernardino Strait, I concentrated Task Force (TF) 38 during the night and steamed north to attack the Northern Force at dawn. I believed that the Center Force had been so heavily damaged in the Sibuyan Sea that it could no longer be considered a serious menace to the Seventh Fleet.

Padding was used to try to confuse the enemy cryptanalysis when sending messages. The padding consisted of removing the first four words and the last three. Admiral Nimitz sent Halsey a message concerning the 7th Fleet. The communications staff correctly removed the first four words but forgot to eliminate the last three. The message delivered to Halsey ended with, "The world wonders." Halsey took this as criticism from Nimitz. He threw his hat to the deck and went into a rage. His chief of staff Rear Admiral Robert Carney confronted him, saying, "Stop it! What the hell's the matter with you? Pull yourself together."

Another factor that might have had an influence on Admiral Halsey was that he was somewhat critical of Admiral Spruance for not chasing the IJN after the battle of the Philippine Sea. However, historians have nothing but praise for Admiral Raymond A. Spruance for his leadership in the battle of the Philippine Sea.

During this time, we of the invasion force were busy unloading troops, equipment, and supplies on the east beaches of the island of Leyte. We were totally unaware that we had very little protection from the IJN southern force. At this point in time, the southern force was unaware that the decoy for the 3rd Fleet had worked and assumed that they were engaging Halsey's third fleet. The Japanese southern force decided to order "general attack," which called for the fleet to split into divisions and attack independently.

This was one of the most courageous battles in the history of naval warfare. Enter the destroyer USS Johnson, which fought with such force that the US Commander Sprague ordered a "small boys attack." Lieutenant Commander

Ernest E. Evans (USS Johnson Commander), on his own initiative and being hopelessly outclassed, directed his ship at full speed into the Japanese fleet, firing his torpedoes. He was followed by the destroyers Hoel and Heermann and the destroyer escort Samuel B. Roberts under the command of Lt. Cdr. Copeland (which earned the title of "the destroyer escort that fought like a battleship") who said to his crew by bullhorn, "This will be a fight against overwhelming odds from which survival could not be expected." The Hoel and the Heermann were hit multiple times and quickly sank. After expending all its torpedoes, the Johnson continued to fight with its five-inch guns until it was sunk by a group of Japanese destroyers. The ferocity of the battle led the Japanese to believe that they were engaging a major fleet rather than mere escort carriers and destroyers. With the confusion of the general attack they previously ordered, the Japanese decided to break off the battle and headed north to regroup. After regrouping and turning again toward Leyte Gulf, the Japanese commander received a message that a group of American carriers were just north of his fleet. Preferring to expend his fleet against capital ships rather than transports, they lost the opportunity to destroy the invasion of Leyte Island. For this, I am eternally grateful.

The United States lost six warships during the battle of Leyte Gulf, while the Japanese lost twenty-six warships. The Japanese faced a serious problem with damaged warships. If they sent them to Singapore, there were inadequate repair facilities. If they went back to Japan, there was scant oil supply.

The IJN had suffered its greatest loss of ships and crew ever. The failure to stop the invasion of Leyte meant the loss of the Philippines, which in turn meant the Japanese would be cut off from their occupied territories in southeast Asia. The resources from this part of Asia were vital to Japan.

The battle for Leyte Gulf had been too large to be ignored with the loss of personnel and ships. The navy decided to put most of the information into an article to be published in *Popular Mechanics*. The article said the battle had gone exactly as Admiral Halsey had planned. It was several years before the true story appeared and became known to the American people.

General MacArthur kept his promise of "I shall return" by wading ashore on D-day. He challenged the Philippine people by addressing them via radio. "People of the Philippines, I have returned," he proclaimed. "The hour of your redemption is here ... rally to me ... as the lines of battle roll forward to bring you within the zone of operation. Rise and strike."

The landing was accomplished with great precision, but the objective was barely visible through the cloak of bursting bombs and projectiles. Our landing craft returned from the beach with twenty-eight wounded army troops and two civilians for treatment by our ship's doctors and corpsman.

The Bell and other APAs in the invasion received a "well done" from Rear Admiral Conolly. We then took aboard the Admiral of the British Fleet Lord Roger Keyes for transport back to Manus in the Admiralty Islands.

Table 15: Troop casualties during the battle for Leyte

	USA	JAPAN
Killed	3,500	70,000
Wounded	11,991	-
Captured	89*	-

* USA Missing

After a trip to New Guinea for making some troop transfers, we arrived back in Manus on November 8. On the morning of November 10, for some unknown reason, Capt. Ritchie moved our anchorage from being next to an ammunition ship, the Mount Hood, to another location. I was working on top deck with the 20mm guns when the Mount Hood exploded. The resulting blast floored all of us who were top side. The result was no survivors on the Mount Hood except the ship's crew sent for mail, and many ships adjacent were sunk or damaged. It was just another close call that followed me throughout my navy career. Tim Churchill expressed our close call in his poem "Deathly Encounters."

Deathly Encounters

Some close calls in my memory still,
When I think back in time,
Like Kamikaze reads I saw,
in ugly war and grime.

Another instance I recall
An ammo ship so near,
It blew itself to kingdom come
and filled my heart with fear.

And then a bad collision came,
two ships collide at sea,
A dreadful night for both the crews
But fortune smiled on me.

A bullet whizzed by left ear,
That left me dazed, in shock;
A thing you don't forget I guess,
It's something carved in rock.

Once while driving in the ALPS,
I missed a crucial curve;
I left the roadway, yet remained,
with very shattered nerve.

At other times and events past,
With dangers on the line,
My close encounters seemed to say,
"Good fortune": has been mine.

After Leyte, the Bell spent considerable time shifting troops and casualties from island to island and finally ended up in San Francisco during the latter part of 1944 for three months of overhaul and repair to get ready for the invasion of Okinawa.

The following were fourteen troop members awarded the Medal of Honor for their actions during the invasion of Leyte. (For a detailed description of why they were awarded this medal, please visit *www.themedalofhonor.org*.)

George Benjamin Jr., born April 24, 1919, in Philadelphia, Pennsylvania
Richard I. Bong, born September 24, 1920, in Poplar, Wisconsin
Leonard C. Brostrom, born November 23, 1920, in Preston, Idaho
Elmer E. Fryar, born February 10, 1914, in Denver, Colorado
Leroy Johnson, born December 6, 1919, in Caney Creek, Louisiana
Ova A. Kelly, born March 27, 1914, in Norwood, Missouri
William A. McWhorter, born December 7, 1918, in Liberty, South Carolina
Harold H. Moon Jr., born March 15, 1921 in Albuquerque, NM
Charles E. Mower, born November 29, 1924, in Chippewa Falls, Wisconsin
Robert P. Nett, born June 13, 1922, in New Haven, Connecticut

Richard H. O'Kane, born February 2, 1911, in Dover, New Hampshire
John F. Thorson, born May 10, 1920, in Armstrong, Iowa
Dirk J. Vlug, born August 20, 1916, in Maple Lake, Minnesota
Francis B. Wai, born April 17, 1917, in Honolulu, Hawaii

THE BATTLE FOR LUZON IN THE PHILIPPINES

I just can't understand how such a damn fool could have gotten to be a general.

—General Eisenhower's comment on General MacArthur in Ann Whitman's diary, December 4, 1954

(Eisenhower admitted that MacArthur was smart, decisive, and a brilliant military mind.)

**The Philippines, showing both Leyte and Luzon
(Courtesy of WorldAtlas)**

When General Eisenhower spoke at London's Guild Hall in June 1945, he said, "Humility must always be the portion of any man who receives acclaim earned in the blood of his followers and the sacrifices of his friends."

Due to the importance of the Philippines and prior to the Japanese attack, the US had on the islands 135,000 troops and 227 aircraft in late 1941. However, the Japanese had captured Luzon, the largest island of the Philippines, in early 1942. Almost immediately after arriving in Australia, MacArthur began promoting the need to recapture the Philippines. This was in direct conflict with Admiral Nimitz and Admiral King. Their argument was that it had to wait until victory was certain. This resulted in MacArthur having to wait for two years to see himself wading ashore on both Leyte and Luzon. The Japanese had controlled the Philippines from May 1942. The defeat of the American forces led to General MacArthur's departure to Australia and General Jonathan Wainwright's capture. General MacArthur made sure that the cameras caught the action of him wading ashore at Leyte on October 20, 1944, and again on January 9, 1945, at Luzon.

The Allies had taken control of the important locations of Luzon by March 1945. However, the Japanese held out in the mountains until the surrender on August 15, 1945. The invasion of Luzon needed a land base of air support to keep in step with the navy's philosophy for land-based air support. After Leyte, the island of Mindoro was invaded. Troops under General William C. Dunckel captured the island, and by

December, two airbases on Mindoro were ready to assist the invasion of Luzon.

The US went to great lengths to convince the Japanese that Luzon would be attacked from the south. For example, dummies were parachuted into the southern area. Minesweepers cleared the bays in the south, and Filipino resistance fighters conducted sabotage operations in southern Luzon. But with all the effort, the Japanese General Yamashita was not fooled, and he built significant defenses in the areas surrounding Lingayen Gulf in Northern Luzon.

The assault was launched on January 9, 1945, with heavy bombardment of Japanese shore positions starting at 7:00, and the landings followed one hour later. The landing force faced heavy opposition from Japanese kamikaze planes. The escort carrier Ommaney Bay was destroyed by the attack along with a destroyer and several other warships.

The army landed about 175,000 troops along a twenty-mile beachhead within a few days. The plan was to drive south toward Clark Field and then on to Manila. Only after completing this phase was the army to push north to control the roads leading into the northern part of Luzon.

While not the highest in US casualties, it was the highest in total casualties in battle during World War II. The result was that nearly 205,000 Japanese combatants were killed. Also, eight thousand US military members were killed, and somewhere between 120,000 to 140,000 Filipino civilians and combatants were killed.

The US forces did not meet much resistance until they reached Clark Air Base on January 23. The battle at that point lasted until the end of January. Then the US launched a second amphibious landing on January 15, which was about forty-five miles southwest of Manila. Then on January 31, two regiments of the 11th Airborne Division made an airborne assault, which allowed an approach from the south. On February 11, 1945, the 11th Airborne Division captured the last Japanese outer defenses, which allowed the US and Filipino forces to circle the whole city of Manila.

Battles continued throughout the island of Luzon for several weeks, and pockets of Japanese soldiers held out in the mountains, but most ceased resistance with the unconditional surrender of the Japanese on August 15, 1945.

Table 16: Troop casualties for Luzon, including POWs

TROOPS	USA	JAPAN	PHILIPPINES
Civilian Killed	-	-	120,000-140,000
Wounded	29,560	-	-
Killed	8310	205,535	-
POW	-	9050	-

The outstanding question in my mind is why every US president since Jimmy Carter has visited Normandy, but only Clinton and Obama have visited the American Memorial Cemetery on Luzon. The US men buried at Normandy total 9,387, but at Manila American Cemetery on Luzon, 17,206 troops are buried. The invasion of Normandy put 73,000 US troops on the Utah and Omaha beaches. The invasion of Luzon put 175,000 troops on a twenty-mile beach head. There are three Medal of Honor recipients at Normandy and twenty-three at the Manila American Cemetery.

Why are the presidents and congressional members so attracted to Normandy? I can only conclude that being close to Paris is more desirable than being close to Manila. This tells me it is not about honoring veterans but more about honoring self.

I have heard all kinds of excuses as to why the European Theater is more popular: we the people of US migrated from Europe, the battles on Luzon and Okinawa occurred when people in the US were getting ready to celebrate the victory in Europe, the death of FDR took the headlines when those battles were being fought. The fact remains that out of all the casualties in World War II, nearly 50 percent were in the Pacific Theater of war, and in my opinion, Midway should be the Pacific Normandy. What those marine and navy pilots did for this country at Midway should never be forgotten.

The following is a list of Medals of Honor awarded during the battle of Luzon. (For a detailed description on why they were awarded this medal, please visit *www.themedalofhonor.org.)*

Thomas E. Adkins, born February 5, 1921, in Campobello, South Carolina

Elmer Charles Bigelow, born July 20, 1920, in Hebron, Illinois

Joseph J. Cicchetti, born June 8, 1923, in Waynesburg, Ohio

Raymond H. Cooley, born May 7, 1914, in Dunlap, Tennessee

George Fleming Davis, born March 23, 1911, in Manila, Philippines

James H. Diamond, born April 22, 1925, in New Orleans, Louisiana

David M. Gonzales, born June 9, 1923, in Pacoima, California

William J. Grabiarz, born March 25, 1925, in Buffalo, New York

Harry R. Harr, born February 22, 1921, in Pine Croft, Pennsylvania

Dexter J. Kerstetter, born December 21, 1907, in Centralia, Washington

Anthony L. Krotiak, born August 15, 1915, in Chicago, Illinois

Robert E. Laws, born January 18, 1921, in Altoona, Pennsylvania

Melvin Mayfield, born March 24, 1919, in Salem, West Virginia

Lloyd G. McCarter, born April 11, 1917, in St. Maries, Idaho

Charles L. McGaha, born February 26, 1914, in Crosby, Tennessee

Thomas B. McGuire Jr., born in Ridgewood, New Jersey

John R. McKinney, born in Woodcliff, Georgia

Laverne Parrish, born in Knox City, Missouri

Manuel Perez Jr., born March 3, 1923, in Oklahoma City, Oklahoma

John N. Reese Jr., born in Muskogee, Oklahoma

Cleto Rodriguez, born in San Marcos, Texas

Donald E. Rudolph, born in South Haven, Minnesota

William R. Shockley, born December 4, 1918, in Bokoshe, Oklahoma

William A. Shomo, born May 30, 1918, in Jeannette, Pennsylvania

John C. Sjogren, born August 16, 1916, in Rockford, Michigan

William H. Thomas, born January 13, 1923, in Wynne, Alaska

Ysmael R. Villegas, born March 21, 1924, in Casa Blanca, California

Robert M. Viale, born April 21, 1916, in Bayside, California

Howard E. Woodford, born June 21, 1921, in Barberton, Ohio

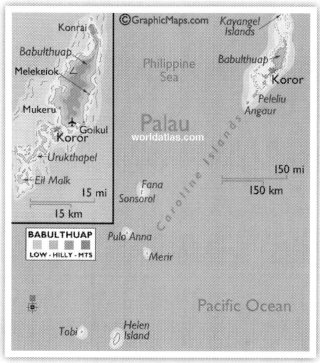

**See upper right for the island of Peleliu—
another step in the ladder toward Japan
(Courtesy of World atlas)**

The battle for Peleliu was fought in the months of September and November 1944. The war in the Pacific brought two different options for winning. The strategy proposed by General MacArthur was to work his way through the Philippines followed by taking Okinawa and then attack the Japanese mainland. Admiral Nimitz favored a more direct route bypassing the Philippines and seizing Okinawa and Taiwan to use as staging areas for the assault on Japan. President Roosevelt traveled to Pearl Harbor to meet with both men to settle the strategy. MacArthur's plan was adopted.

After their repeated losses throughout the Pacific, the Japanese adopted a new strategy whereby they would allow the US troops to reach the beach with little resistance, but then, through carefully placed bunkers and artillery with tunnels connecting these positions, they would inflict heavy losses to American troops. This, the Japanese thought, would force the US more into a war of attrition requiring more and more resources.

The Japanese defenses were based on Peleliu's highest point, the Umurbrogol Mountain. It was a collection of hills and steep ridges located at the center of the Island. This mountain contained more than five hundred caves that were connected by tunnels. Many of the tunnels were mine shafts turned into defense positions.

The battle with the Japanese troops around Umurbrogol Mountain is considered the most difficult military battle encountered during World War II. After this battle, the 1st Marine Division was so depleted with casualties that it did not see action again until the battle for Okinawa.

Also, the battle became controversial due to the island's strategic value, as the airfield became unnecessary, and it was never used as a staging area for future battles. However, that is twenty/twenty hindsight, because no one thought the battle would be as tough as it was. In fact, it was predicted by a marine officer that the battle would be over in three days with little resistance from the Japanese.

Table 17: Troop casualties that occurred during the battle for Peleliu

	USA	JAPAN
Killed	1,794	10,695-10,999
Wounded	8,010	-0
Captured	-0	202

The battle for Peleliu resulted in eight of the nation's highest awards, the Medal of Honor. Those selected were the following individuals.

Lewis K. Bausell, born April 17, 1924, in Pulaski, Virginia
Arthur J. Jackson, born October 18, 1924, in Cleveland, Ohio

Richard E. Kraus, born November 24, 1925, in Chicago, Illinois. Unhesitatingly volunteering for the extremely hazardous mission of evacuating a wounded comrade from the front lines, Pfc. Kraus and three companions courageously made their way forward and successfully penetrated the lines for some distance before the enemy opened with an intense, devastating barrage of hand grenades that forced the stretcher party to take cover and subsequently abandon the mission. While returning to the rear, they observed two men approaching who appeared to be marines and immediately demanded the password. When, instead of answering, one of the two Japanese threw a hand grenade into the midst of the group, Pfc. Kraus heroically flung himself upon the grenade and, covering it with his body, absorbed the full impact of the explosion and was instantly killed. By his prompt action and great personal valor in the face of almost certain death, he saved the lives of his three companions.

John D. New, born in Mobile, Alabama
Wesley Phelps, born June 12, 1923, in Neafus, Kentucky
Everett P. Pope, born July 16, 1919, in Milton, Massachusetts
Charles H. Roan, born August 16, 1923, in Claude, Texas
Carlton R. Rouh, born May 11, 1919, in Lindenwood, New Jersey

THE BATTLE FOR THE ISLAND OF IWO JIMA

Among the men who fought on Iwo Jima, uncommon valor was a common virtue.

—Admiral Chester Nimitz

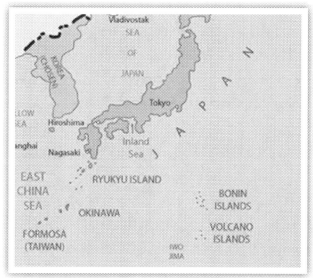

The battle for Iwo Jima, a steppingstone
toward Okinawa and a base for fighter
aircraft to escort the B-29 raids on Japan
(Courtesy of Worldatlas)

The battle for Iwo Jima was fought in February and March of 1945. Iwo Jima was another step closer to Japanese mainland and had three airfields that would be of great value for land-based aircraft for the invasion on Okinawa. Critics question the need, especially after the heavy losses to US troops at Peleliu. But to me, that is second-guessing and is not in agreement with the original philosophy of "up the ladder a step at a time." The Japanese were using this base for fighter aircraft to intercept the air raids being flown from Saipan and Tinian by our new long-range bombers, the B-29s. With the capture of this Island and its air bases, we could then provide fighter escort for the B-29s on their bombing raids to and from Tokyo.

Iwo Jima was the only battle in the Pacific where our losses (killed and wounded) were greater than those of the Japanese. The battle and the victory by the US were assured from the start, because the Japanese had nowhere to retreat and no possibility of reinforcement or supplies due to the US being in control of the air and sea surrounding Iwo Jima. Basically, the Japanese were fighting there as a delaying tactic to buy time for the homeland defenses to get well-established for the obvious invasion of the homeland, which was fast approaching. The commander of the Japanese forces on Iwo Jima used the same philosophy that was used on Peleliu: do not try to stop the landing at the beach but build a strong defense with heavy weapons of machine guns and artillery at strategic locations. As a result, hundreds of bunkers, pillboxes, and tunnels connecting the network were placed all over the island. This included hidden artillery and mortars positioned along with land mines.

The Japanese allowed the first wave of marines to reach a certain point and then opened fire from the concealed bunkers and firing positions. The first wave took devastating losses from the machine guns. The Japanese also attacked with heavy artillery from their position on Mount Suribachi.

The marines soon realized that firearms were relatively ineffective against the Japanese defenders and relied mostly on flamethrowers and hand grenades. Also, the tunnel system was difficult to overcome, because once clearing a bunker with a flame thrower or grenade and moving on, the Japanese would reoccupy through the tunnel connections and come at the marines from the rear as they advanced. An additional problem with using the flamethrower was the very short range, requiring the person using it to be very close and often exposed to enemy fire.

Mount Suribachi is the dominant geographical feature on the Island of Iwo Jima and became world-famous from the photograph taken by Joe Rosenthal on February 23, 1945. It depicts five marines and a navy corpsman raising the flag of the US atop Mount Suribachi. The fact that the photograph is that of a second flag raising caused some to say it was staged. The first flag was a much smaller flag. The real story is as follows.

It so happened that the Secretary of the Navy James Forrestal had decided to go ashore and witness the fight for Mount Suribachi. After seeing the flag flying above the mountain, he decided he wanted it for a souvenir. The commander of the marines who put the flag there said, "Hell, no. That flag belongs to the battalion." So, the commander sent a marine to get another flag, and at the last minute, he said to make it a bigger one. It was the second flag that Rosenthal snapped that caught the eye of the world. He said he had set his camera down, and out of the corner of his eye, he saw the flag going up, so he grabbed the camera, turned, and snapped. It became the only photograph in history to win the Pulitzer Prize for photography in the same year it was taken.

Two of my favorite entertainers in show business were Johnny Carson and Lee Marvin. But I have to say I was offended by the fabricated story they told on the *Tonight Show* about Lee's action and that of Captain Kangaroo (Bob Keeshan) during the battle for Iwo Jima. The truth according to *snopes.com* is that neither was ever on Iwo Jima, and neither was awarded the Navy Cross. Lee did get the Purple Heart for being wounded on Saipan, and Bob Keeshan joined the Marines—but too late to see any action in the Pacific during World War II.

When I think of the 464 Medals of Honor awarded during WWII (and by my count 197 in the Pacific Theater of war), with 266 being awarded posthumously, bravery and claims for medals not awarded is not something to joke about. People such as John Basilone, Richard Kraus, and Richard Fleming and the 263 others who gave their life for their country make joking about Medals of Honor awarded off-limits.

Table 18: Troop and aircraft carrier casualties that occurred for the battle of Iwo Jima

TROOP	USA	Japan	Other
Killed	6,821	18,844	-
Wounded	19,217	-	-
Captured	-	216	3000**

** Japanese soldiers missing

Carrier	USA	JAPAN
Escort Carrier	1	

The following were awarded the Medal of Honor for their actions during the battle of Iwo Jima. (For a detailed description of why they received the award, go to *www.themedalofhonor.org*.)

Charles Joseph Berry, born July 10, 1923, in Lorain, Ohio

William R. Caddy, born August 8, 1925, in Quincy, Massachusetts

Justice M. Chambers, born February 2, 1908, in Huntington, West Virginia

Darrell Samuel Cole, born July 20, 1920, in Flat River, Missouri

Robert H. Dunlap, born October 19, 1920, in Abingdon, Illinois

Ross F. Gray, born August 1920 in Marvel Valley, Alabama

William G. Harrell, born October 2, 1923, in Quiet Dell, West Virginia

Rufus G. Herring, born June 11, 1921, in Roseboro, North Carolina

Douglas T. Jacobson, born November 25, 1925, in Rochester, New York

Joseph Rodolph Julian, born April 3, 1918, in Sturbridge, Massachusetts

James D. La Belle, born November 22, 1925, in Columbia Heights, Minnesota

John H. Leims, born June 8, 1921, in Chicago, Illinois

Jacklyn H. Lucas, born February 14, 1928, in Plymouth, North Carolina

Jack Lummus, born October 22, 1915, in Ennie, Texas

Harry L. Martin, born January 4, 1911, in Bucyrus, Ohio

Joseph J. McCarthy, born August 11, 1911, in Chicago, Illinois

George Phillips, born July 14, 1926, in Rick Hill, Missouri

Francis J. Pierce, born December 7, 1924, in Earlville, Iowa

Donald J. Ruhl, born July 2, 1923, in Columbus, Montana

Franklin E. Sigler, born September 30, 1921, in Dayton, Ohio. Voluntarily taking command of his rifle squad when the leader became a casualty, Pvt. Sigler fearlessly led a bold charge against an enemy gun installation that had held up the advance of his company for several days and, reaching the position in advance of the others, assailed the emplacement with hand grenades and personally annihilated the entire crew. As additional Japanese troops opened fire from concealed tunnels and caves above, he quickly scaled the rocks leading to the attacking guns, surprised the enemy with a furious one-man assault, and although severely wounded in the encounter, he deliberately crawled back to his squad position, where he steadfastly refused evacuation, persistently directing heavy machine gun and rocket barrages on the Japanese cave entrances. Undaunted by the merciless rain of hostile fire during the intensified action, he gallantly disregarded his own painful wounds to aid casualties, carrying three wounded squad members to safety behind the lines and returning to continue the battle with renewed determination until ordered to retire for medical treatment.

Tony Stein, born September 30, 1921, in Dayton, Ohio. First man of his unit to be on station after hitting the beach in the initial assault, Cpl. Stein, armed with a personally improvised aircraft-type weapon, provided rapid covering fire as the remainder of his platoon attempted to move into position. When his comrades were stalled by a concentrated machine gun and mortar barrage, he gallantly stood upright and exposed himself to the enemy's view, thereby drawing the hostile fire to his own person and enabling him to observe the location of the furiously blazing hostile guns. Determined to neutralize the strategically placed weapons, he boldly charged the enemy pillboxes one by one and succeeded in killing twenty of the enemy during the furious single-handed assault. Cool and courageous under the merciless hail of exploding shells and bullets that fell on all sides, he continued to deliver the fire of his skillfully improvised weapon at a tremendous rate of speed that rapidly exhausted his ammunition. Undaunted, he removed his helmet and shoes to expedite his movements and ran back to the beach for additional ammunition, making a total of eight trips under intense fire and carrying or assisting a wounded man back each time. Despite the unrelenting savagery and confusion of battle, he rendered prompt assistance to his platoon whenever the unit was in position, directing the fire of a halftrack against a stubborn pillbox until he had affected the ultimate destruction of the Japanese fortification. Later in the day, although his weapon was twice shot from his hands, he personally covered the withdrawal of his platoon to the company position.

George E. Wahlen, born August 8, 1924, in Ogden, Utah
William Gary Walsh, born April 7, 1922, in Roxbury, Massachusetts
Wilson D. Watson, born February 18, 1921, in Tuscumbia, Alabama
Hershel W. Williams, born October 2, 1923, in Quiet Dell, West Virginia
Jack Williams, born October 18, 1924, in Harrison, Alaska
John H. Willis, born June 10, 1921, in Columbia, Tennessee

THE BATTLE FOR OKINAWA

Let us pray that peace be now restored to the world and that God will preserve it always.

—General Douglas MacArthur, Supreme Allied Commander of South West Pacific (1945)

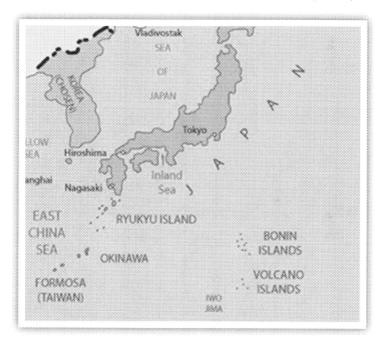

The battle for Okinawa put the US on the doorstep for the invasion of Japan, the last rung in the ladder in the march to the Japanese homeland. (Courtesy of World Atlas)

The battle for Okinawa lasted eighty-two days and was fought from April until mid-June 1945. With this island in hand, the US would be only about 340 miles from the Japanese mainland, and Okinawa would serve as one of the bases for the invasion of Japan. The battle for Okinawa would come to represent the highest casualties of all the battles in the Pacific Theater of war. Government sources from Okinawa report a total of 77,166 Japanese soldiers who were killed or committed suicide. The US and its allies suffered total casualties of 65,000, with 14,009 killed. At the same time, it is estimated that between 42,000 and 150,000 local civilians were either killed or committed suicide.

The USS J. Franklin Bell left San Francisco on February 28, 1945, for the final battle of WWII (Okinawa). I remember it well, because on board, after loading officers and troops in Pearl Harbor, were eighteen army nurses. All the enlisted men were restricted to the lower decks. We assumed that the officers did not want any competition. After a short stop at Eniwetok, we went on to Saipan, where all the passengers were unloaded. The Bell then headed for Noumea, New Caledonia. The reason I remember this trip is because our top speed was about ten knots as a result of the loss of power in one of the turbines. At that speed, we were sitting ducks for Japanese submarines, but the trip was uneventful. After repairs were made, we spent time transferring troops between Guadalcanal, Ulithi Atoll, and Eniwetok.

This battle at Okinawa was not the first time the Japanese used the kamikaze tactics, but it was the first time they were used as a defensive measure. (Kamikazes were first used in the battle of Leyte Gulf.) Between April and May 1945, there were seven major kamikaze attacks involving more than 1,500 planes. We were also aware of the possibility of suicide boats, and this created an experience that I will never forget. I was in one of our LCVPs, creating smoke along with another gunner's mate, a coxswain and a naval officer. We were one of several boats to lay a smoke screen to hide the ships from Japanese planes. If we were challenged, we had a special light to give as a response. It so happened that in the thick of smoke, we came upon a US gunboat, and when attempting to answer the challenge, the light was dropped by our officer, whereupon the gunboat opened fire with small caliber guns. We all went to the bilges, and fortunately, the officer found the light and gave signal to stop the shooting. The gunboat turned out to be on its first action of the war and was very apologetic about having fired on us. The crew members welcomed us aboard and treated us like royalty.

At Okinawa, the Bell anchored in Hagushi, Anchorage, and unloaded our troops—a US Naval Construction Battalion. The Japanese planes dropped four bombs on the first day that were near misses. The only casualty was William Wrenn, who received facial wounds while serving in one of our smoke boats. The wound was not life-threatening. The Bell remained at Okinawa for several days and was subject to numerous air raids.

I wrote the following is article for a newspaper after our visit to Okinawa. It describes my views seventy-two years after D-day 1945.

> It is on to Okinawa but with some regret because
> the Chamorros, who inhabit the island of Saipan,
> were so friendly and grateful that America gave

them their freedom. Janice said she had thought all these years that our US soldiers were in the South Pacific just to defend America. However, during this trip we both became aware that US soldiers were also there to liberate the island people of the South Pacific. And they are so grateful for that. I had the urge to just stay and enjoy the handshakes and hugs that flowed so freely. The Battle for Okinawa was fought from the beginning of April to mid-June 1945. There were two other major events during this time that reduced the public awareness of the intensity of this battle: the celebration for VE day in Europe and the death of President Roosevelt.

These events were but one more reason for me to write *Forgotten Warriors.*

The Japanese had initiated the Kamikaze attack at Leyte, and it became one of their most important weapons at Okinawa. Admiral Spruance began the battle with the Cruiser Indianapolis as his flagship. After taking a direct hit by the Kamikaze he switched to the battleship Mew Mexico which was also hit by a Kamikaze. I think his comment that "Okinawa was his toughest experience of the war" was justified.

Another ship, the destroyer Laffey, faced 22 suicide planes in a little more than an hour. Six of the planes hit the ship but the destroyer survived.

My initial responsibility during the battle was to lay a smoke screen covering the bay to hide the ships. We escaped quite well with only one wounded sailor out of our group.

After this phase of smoke screening was over, I went back to be the Gun Captain on the aft 40mm anti-aircraft gun on the USS J. Franklin Bell. Our goal was to shoot the enemy down before they could fly into a ship.

The bay where I helped lay the smoke screen to protect ships from the Japanese kamikaze planes (Courtesy of D. Ralph Young, public domain)

The Kamikazes sunk 19 ships; damaged 181 ships; killed 5,000 and wounded more than 10,000 of US servicemen in this entire battle.

While on the island, our tour group visited Hacksaw Ridge and listened to our guide tell us about the many liberties the director of the movie took as related to what really

Standing By The Rock Where Desmond Doss Lowered The Wounded Comrades. (Courtesy- D Ralph Young -Public Domain)

happened. But nothing the movie portrayed took away from the heroic work of Desmond Doss who was awarded to Medal of Honor for his action. Desmond Doss lowered the wounded men over Hacksaw Ridge right behind the rock where we are standing.

Of course, the fence was a later addition.

Huge cave where 1,600 natives were hiding (Courtesy of D. Ralph Young, public domain)

We also visited the many caves used during the war. Some were in the jungle and others in populated areas such as the Japanese Naval Command which was deeply underground and held many passages.

Our guide told us the story of how 1600 natives were hiding in a cave for over 90 days and would not come out when our US Marines called for them to do so. Finally, one native came out with his hands up saying, "Don't shoot." He told the American soldiers that he had been an island soldier and that he knew the people inside the cave were afraid of the Americans because of the propaganda they had received. He requested a little more time with the frightened natives so he could convince them to come out and be rescued. Additional time was granted, and the island soldier was credited with saving the lives of 1600 people.

It was a great trip for Janice and me, sponsored by **Beyond Band of Brothers**, a Tour Group based in Budapest, Hungary with a satellite office in Lexington, Kentucky. I enjoyed every minute.

D Ralph Young

THE STORY OF DESMOND T. DOSS

Desmond Doss was born February 1919 in Lynchburg, Virginia. He did not oppose the war effort, but he refused to kill and therefore would not fire a gun. This created all kinds of trouble with the hardnosed Sgt. and officers. After a long battle, he finally won on the basis that he would serve as a medic. His action during battle has been made into a movie called *Hacksaw Ridge* produced by Mel Gibson. For his action during battle, please read his complete citation.

Desmond T. Doss, born February 7, 1919, in Lynchburg, Virginia. He was a company aid man when the 1st Battalion assaulted a jagged escarpment four hundred feet high. As our troops gained the summit, a heavy concentration of artillery, mortar, and machine gun fire crashed into them, inflicting approximately seventy-five casualties and driving the others back. Pfc. Doss refused to seek cover and remained in the fire-swept area with the many stricken, carrying them one by one to the edge of the escarpment and there lowering them on a rope-supported litter down the face of a cliff to friendly hands. On May 2, he exposed himself to heavy rifle and mortar fire in rescuing a wounded man two hundred yards forward of the lines on the same escarpment; two days later, he treated four men who had been cut down while assaulting a strongly defended cave, advancing through a shower of grenades to within eight yards of enemy forces in a cave's mouth, where he dressed his comrades' wounds before making four separate trips under fire to evacuate them to safety. On May 5, he unhesitatingly braved enemy shelling and small arms fire to assist an artillery officer.

He applied bandages, moved his patient to a spot that offered protection from small arms fire, and while artillery and mortar shells fell close by, painstakingly administered plasma. Later that day, when an American was severely wounded by fire from a cave, Pfc. Doss crawled to him where he had fallen twenty-five feet from the enemy position, rendered aid, and carried him one hundred yards to safety while continually exposed to enemy fire. On May 21, in a night attack on high ground near Shuri, he remained in exposed territory. While the rest of his company took cover, he fearlessly risked the chance that he would be mistaken for an infiltrating Japanese soldier and gave aid to the injured until he was himself seriously wounded in the legs by the explosion of a grenade. Rather than call another aid man, he cared for his own injuries and waited five hours before litter bearers reached him and started _carrying him to cover. The trio was caught in an enemy tank attack, and Pfc. Doss, seeing a more critically wounded man nearby, crawled off the litter and directed the bearers to give their first attention to the other man. Awaiting the litter bearers' return, he was again struck, this time suffering a compound fracture of his arm. With magnificent fortitude, he bound a rifle stock to his shattered arm as a splint and then crawled three hundred yards over rough terrain to the aid station.

Table 19: Troop, ship, carrier, and artillery casualties during the invasion of Okinawa

·TROOPS	USA	JAPAN
Killed	12,000	77,166-110,000
Wounded	31-40,000	7,000+
Captured	-	30,000

*30,000 Non Combat losses

SHIPS/CARRIERS/ARTILERY	USA	JAPAN
Ships	38	16
Aircraft	763	7800
Tanks	225	27
Artillery Pieces	-	743

The battle for Okinawa resulted in twenty-two of the nation's highest award: the Medal of Honor. The following individuals were selected. (For details on others who received the award, go to www.themedalofhonor.org)

Beauford T. Anderson, born July 6, 1922, in Eagle, Wisconsin

Richard E. Bush, born December 23, 1923, in Glasgow, Kentucky. Bush showed conspicuous gallantry and intrepidity at the risk of his life above and beyond the call of duty as a squad leader serving with the 1st Battalion, 4th Marines, 6th Marine Division in action against Japanese forces during the final assault against Mount Yaetake on Okinawa, Ryukyu Islands, April 16, 1945. Rallying his men forward with indomitable determination, Cpl. Bush boldly defied the slashing fury of concentrated Japanese artillery fire pouring down from the gun-studded mountain fortress to lead his squad up the face of the rocky precipice, sweep over the ridge, and drive the defending troops from their deeply entrenched position. With his unit, the first to break through to the inner defense of Mount Yaetake, he fought relentlessly in the forefront of the action until seriously wounded, and he evacuated with others under protecting rocks. Although prostrate under medical treatment when a Japanese hand grenade landed in the midst of the group, Cpl. Bush, alert and courageous in extremity as in battle, unhesitatingly pulled the deadly missile to himself and absorbed the shattering violence of the exploding charge in his body, thereby saving his fellow marines from severe injury or death despite the certain peril to his own life. By his valiant leadership and aggressive tactics in the face of savage opposition, Cpl. Bush contributed materially to the success of the sustained drive toward the conquest of this fiercely defended outpost of the Japanese empire. His constant concern for the welfare of his men, his resolute spirit of self-sacrifice, and his unwavering devotion to duty throughout the bitter conflict enhance and sustain the highest traditions of the US Naval Service.

Robert Eugene Bush, born October 4, 1926, in Tacoma, Washington
Henry A. Courtney, born January 6, 1916, in Duluth, Minnesota
Clarence B. Craft, born in San Bernardino, California
James Day, born October 5, 1925, in East St. Louis, Illinois
John P. Fardy, born August 8, 1922, in Chicago, Illinois
William A. Foster, born February 17, 1915, in Cleveland, Ohio

Harold Gonsalves, born January 28, 1926, in Alameda, California

Dale Merlin Hansen, born December 13, 1922, in Wisner, Nebraska

Louis James Hauge Jr., born December 12, 1924, in Ada, Minnesota

Elbert Luther Kinser, born October 21, 1922, in Greenville, Tennessee

Fred Faulkner Lester, born April 29, 1926, in Downers Grove, Illinois

Martin O'May, born April 18, 1922, in Phillipsburg, New Jersey

John Meagher, born December 5, 1917, in Jersey City, New Jersey

Richard Miles McCool, born January 4, 1922, in Tishomingo, Oklahoma

Robert Miller McTureous Jr., born March 26, 1924, in Altoona, Florida

Edward J. Moskala, born November 6, 1921, in Chicago, Illinois

Joseph E. Muller, born June 23, 1908, in Holyoke, Massachusetts

Lejandro R. Renteria Ruiz, born June 23, 1923, in Loving, New Mexico

Albert Earnest Schwab, born July 17, 1920, in Washington, District of Columbia

Seymour W. Terry, born December 11, 1918, in Little Rock, Arkansas

The next section portrays the history of the USS J. Franklin Bell as well as her retirement from active naval service.

THE USS J. FRANKLIN BELL, HER HISTORY AND DEMISE

I know not with what World War III will be fought, but World War IV will be fought with sticks and stones.

—Albert Einstein

The Bell camouflaged to avoid
detection by the enemy
(Courtesy of Military Archives, public domain)

The J. Franklin Bell was a Harris class attack transport ship. She was built in 1921 and served in the merchant service for twenty years. The ship was acquired by the army in 1940 and transferred to the navy shortly after Pearl Harbor. The army renamed the ship J. Franklin Bell in honor of the Army Chief of Staff 1906–1910. General Bell was also a Medal of Honor winner for bravery during the Luzon campaign in the Philippines. He grew up on a farm just outside Shelbyville,

Kentucky. So, I was proud to have served on the J. Franklin Bell for more than one reason. Another poem, "The Spirit of the J. Franklin Bell" by Timothy Churchill, expresses the thoughts of all of us who served aboard the Bell. The role of all APAs during World War II was to pick up troops, carry them to the island selected, and then land them on the beaches together with equipment, armament, and supplies.

To aid in the unloading, each ship would supply a beach party that exited the ship and traveled to the beach with the troops to aid in the flow of battle supplies and equipment as well as maintaining the guns and landing craft. This ship policy is why I was sent to the beach at Saipan and Tinian.

Also, in the fall of 1945, the USS J. Franklin Bell was called into service to help move people along the coast of California, as the surface transportation facilities were inadequate to handle the large increase in movement of people and troops up and down the coast. The proud history of the USS J. Franklin Bell included seven battle stars for Aleutians (with landings at Adak, Attu, and Kiska), Tarawa, Kwajalein, Saipan, Tinian, Leyte, and Okinawa.

During the war, the Bell had to dodge torpedoes, outmaneuver bombs, battle strafing planes, hide from kamikaze planes, and survive friendly fire, such as the accidental explosion of the Mount Hood. All this heroic action came to an embarrassing end. As a band played and many guests stood on the dock to meet the troops she was carrying, the Bell crashed into the dock. Fortunately, there were no injuries except to the egos of her crew. We, as its proud shipmates, take some comfort in the fact that in every case when a ship comes into a harbor, a pilot who knows the channels is brought aboard to guide the ship into dock. The local reported the cause as engine failure.

Timothy Churchill describes our feelings about the USS J. Franklin Bell quite well in the following poem.

Farewell Salute to the Bell

A Valiant ship we all once knew
"J. Franklin Bell" by name
With battle scars from World War Two
Awash in victory fame

A ship that served her country well
Composed of steel and men
A ship that sailed right into hell
And lived to fight again

At last, triumphant, homeward bound
Her brave crew through with war
She suffered one last fateful round
At San Francisco's shore.

Her mission ended suddenly,
With holes ripped in her fore
Her brave crew knew, unhappily
The Bell would sail no more

Alas, the decades took their toll;
Brave men who sailed The Bell
Whose names adorn the Honor Roll
Remember here as well,

But to survivors, we now toast,
J. Franklin Bell be praised,
The memories we all can share,
Once more, with glasses raised

After this accident, the USS *J. Franklin Bell* was sent to Suisun Bay, California, and on March 20, 1946, she was decommissioned. She was sold for scrap on April 3, 1948, to the Boston Metals of Baltimore, Maryland.

Listed below are the commanding officers of the USS *J. Franklin Bell* during the war in the Pacific:

- **Captain Herbert J. Grassie** USN April 2–November 2, 1942
- **Captain John B. McGovern** USN November 2, 1942–October 22, 1943
- **Captain Oliver H. Ritchie** USNR October 22, 1943–end of war

The Spirit of the J. Franklin Bell

I am the spirit of a ship, the USS J. Franklin Bell,
I live in the hearts and minds of men;
Men who served on my decks and fired my guns,
And who guided me through troubled waters.

I was born in the time of peace, and calm before the storm;
My decks carried travelers, revelers, and students of the east;
The flag at my mast was red white and blue,
The country I served was a beacon of light for the world.

My mission changed drastically with my nation attacked,
I was filled with combatants and ordered to war;
I was fitted with hardware, munitions and men of steel,
My decks were then trodden by heroes, waiting to die.

There was no glory in war, but my crewmates stood tall,
Defending our nation with courage, determined to win;
They sailed me through storms, battles, torpedoes and bombs,
They gave me more men, with the mission
to fight, and for some, to die.

I was brought to the gates of hell, with troops assaulting the shore,
I scoured the beaches with cannon, and brave men who died;
I met the enemy, with smoke on the water, and fire in the sky.
And I lived to see victory, preserving freedom for my country.

My crewmates have gone now, my guns are
silent; and my engines are still,
And the world is now different, with new dangers, and different foes;
My decks no longer exist, to support a new crop on heroes,
The memories of what we did will soon be gone … Forever.

LIFE ONBOARD SHIP DURING WWII

People often ask what it was like to serve onboard a ship during wartime. Since I was an enlisted man, I cannot describe life for an officer, but it was obvious that officers had more privacy, better meals, and more free time.

For us seamen not on watch (duty station ready for combat, which usually lasted four hours each day), we had to be ready for General Quarters, which always occurred an hour before dusk and again an hour before dawn. This was when the enemy was most likely to attack. The time from midnight to 4:00 a.m. was the most hated period for having to stand watch, because after just getting to sleep, it was time for General Quarters. During the day, we worked at whatever duty we had been assigned. For example, I had been assigned to be a gunner's mate, so I worked on cleaning and lubricating guns, chipping paint, and painting the gun emplacements. Saltwater enhanced corrosion, so chipping and painting were constant chores, as was swabbing decks.

For pastimes, we played cards, read books, wrote letters, watched movies when available (which was not too often), or just visited with friends. We were always looking for some reason to have a special event. The one I remember best was crossing the equator. Those who had never crossed were known as pollywogs. After crossing, a pollywog became a shellback. But to become one, you had to be initiated into that society. The USS J. Franklin Bell had long canvas funnels used to send air below decks when we had troops aboard. The shellbacks saved the garbage for days, and using a funnel that was laid out on the deck, they filled it with the garbage and required each pollywog to crawl through the mess. Those who tried to raise up to avoid crawling through the garbage in the funnel were hit in the butt with a club by the shellbacks stationed along the length of the funnel. When the pollywogs finally reached the end of the funnel, there was King Neptune sitting on his throne, who was the shellback with the biggest belly on the ship. Each pollywog was required to kiss his navel, which covered with hair recovered from the barbershop and soaked in wintergreen. The lips of newly initiated shellbacks burned for days.

Officers did not escape this ritual, and in some cases, it was a chance to get even. For example, we had an officer who never saw a fog nozzle (the brass control at the end of a water hose) that did not need cleaning, regardless of how many times it had been cleaned or how much it shined. So, he was put on four-hour watch in the crow's nest with two fog nozzles instead of binoculars.

It was fun and a diversion from a daily routine of war life in the middle of the Pacific. New shellbacks prayed for at least one more crossing to initiate other pollywogs.

There was only one galley for the whole ship, and when we were carrying combat troops, the chow lines were endless. I am just thankful that the ship's crew had special access. And I did not have to wait, but I always felt sorry for the army and marine troops who we often carried into combat.

The food was pretty good. But the coffee was terrible, and as a result, most of the divisions like us in the ordnance division had a hot plate stashed away in a locker and brewed our own coffee. I had a hard time getting used to navy beans for breakfast, but I must admit that after two years, I started looking forward to Wednesday, because that was navy bean day.

Our greatest fears were not necessarily the Japanese but the surprise, unscheduled, spur-of-the-moment ship inspections. This meant that seamen had to open their lockers, lower their bunks, and wait for the inspection team to pass through the crew quarters. Only those on duty at the time were exempt from the inspection. All kinds of things went on during this period. One group was making "home brew" in the engine room where the warm temperatures enhanced the brew time. The group had a scheme whereby they managed to fall in behind the inspection team carrying their brew, and with a lot of lookouts along the way, they made their way back to the engine room undetected. Alcohol was not allowed on board for enlisted men.

The crew's quarters were two bunks high, and each had a full-length locker. A shower was centrally located to serve several groups. We almost always had freshwater showers. But occasionally, we had to put up with saltwater showers. At this time, if we had a thunderstorm with rain, the announcement would come over the PA system: "All men desiring a freshwater shower, come topside with soap and towel." The troop quarters were different, as they had to sleep in bunks four deep that provided little space between bunks.

I had another freighting experience that I will never forget. Huelen Watts, a gunner's mate from Cullman, Alabama, was my best friend onboard the ship. It was decided that the ammunition storage room needed painting, and Huelen and I volunteered. Access to the room was by ladder and an elevator that was about four feet square. The purpose of the elevator was to send ammunition for the guns, which were located directly above. We almost always used the elevator rather than the several flights by ladder. On one occasion, when I was in the ammunition room by myself, I decided to go topside. So, I got in the elevator and reached around the opening to push the button to send it elevator upward. I immediately discovered that someone had bolted down the hatch at the top of the elevator.

My first thought was of being crushed against the steel hatch that was bolted down, because the normal run stopped about a foot from the top. But I remembered that there was a switch on one side of the elevator shaft that stopped the upward motion. However, I could not remember which side. So, to this day, I do not know how I could have covered all four sides of the elevator with two arms, but I did, and I am surer than ever that it was the result of my mother's prayers. About forty-five minutes later, a sailor walking by the hatch heard my tapping and opened the hatch. I never again started the elevator without looking up to see if there was daylight.

After Okinawa, we headed for Guadalcanal, but the destination was changed in route to Espiritu Santo. Then, after a stop in Noumea, New Caledonia, the USS *J. Franklin Bell* was on its way home—only to hit one of the worst storms the Bell ever experienced. Waves were coming over the bridge, which was about seventy-five feet from the normal water line. When the bow of the ship would go down into a troth created by the waves, the screws would come out of the water, and it was like hitting a brick wall. Those eating in the galley had to hold their trays with one hand and eat with the other. The sad part is that we lost two passengers who disobeyed orders not to go topside, and they were washed overboard.

For those who think the US use of the atomic bomb was a mistake, please consider the fact that about the only Japanese survivors were the ones knocked unconscious or wounded to the point that they could not commit suicide. So, there was no reason to expect them to surrender.

Purple Hearts were awarded on the battlefield, and the US, in preparation for the invasion of Japan, had 1,500,000 Purple Hearts made. If the ratio of three to one held for wounded to killed, then we could have expected about five hundred thousand soldiers to be killed. That is pretty good justification for using the bomb on Hiroshima and Nagasaki. I consider dropping the bomb especially justified since the losses because of the atomic bombs befell the ones that started the war.

After arriving in San Francisco and unloading passengers, the Bell went to pier 62 for about seven weeks of repair. During this period, word was received on August 15, 1945 that the Japanese had surrendered. With repairs made, the ship then went to Seattle, where I served on shore patrol for a few weeks.

In November 1945, I was sent home on home leave and told to report to Louisville, Kentucky to be discharged on December 15. However, when I went to Louisville, my records were not there. So, I was sent home again and told to report back on January 6, 1946. This time, I was discharged from the navy.

It felt strange to be back to free life without being ordered to stand watch or have General Quarters every night at dusk and morning at sunrise. I was just free to do my own thing. The most difficult part was the realization that I did not have a home to call my own. With the passing of my mother during the war, my older brother Vernon and his family of eleven children had moved in with my father. I was left without a home. Therefore, my oldest brother Preston, his wife Florence, and his family of Alice, Preston Jr., and Coleman became like close family, because they allowed me to move in with them.

It also took time to adjust to all the world's changes in 1945, such as the death of President Roosevelt and the new President Harry S. Truman. The Dow Jones high and low for the year were 195 and 155, unemployment was at a low of 1.9 percent, and a postage stamp cost $0.03. One could buy a women's fur coat for $70 and a man's dress shirt for $2.50. The USS Indianapolis, which had just delivered parts needed for the atomic bomb to the island of Tinian, was sunk with the loss of 883 seamen.

THE SINKING OF THE CRUISER USS INDIANAPOLIS

We on the USS *J. Franklin* Bell considered the USS Indianapolis our hero, because in record time, it delivered the triggering device to Tinian that resulted in Japan's surrender in August 1945. The sinking of the Indianapolis resulted in the greatest loss of life by a single ship in the history of the US navy. The name of the cruiser comes from the city of Indianapolis, Indiana, and the ship has a storied past. It hosted President Roosevelt on three different occasions. The last was a tour of South America, where the president said he survived the two-day initiation crossing the equator and became full-fledged shellback.

The Indianapolis served in many battles and was Admiral Spruance's flagship during the battle of the Philippine Sea. For all of us veterans of the Pacific, we considered the record speed trip from San Francisco to Pearl Harbor and on to Tinian with the Uranium-235 that was used to trigger the atomic bomb for Hiroshima to be the most important action of all WWII engagements for this ship. This was the beginning of the end for WWII. It was predicted that we would have lost more than a million personnel with a land invasion of Japan. So, to us veterans fighting in the Pacific, the use of the A-bomb was welcome and justified.

It is sad to think that three hundred crew members went down with the ship because she sank in just twelve minutes. Even sadder is the realization what the nearly nine hundred who made it into the water had to do to survive and live through before being rescued. Only 317 were found alive in the water. They were exposed to the heat, thirst, and hallucinations that compelled them to drink seawater and die from salt poisoning. It is thought that up to 150 were attacked and killed by sharks, the most aggressive being the oceanic whitetip sharks.

The navy initially said that no distress calls were received by any station, ship, or plane. However, a later declassified record showed that three signals were received, but no one acted upon them. One commander was drunk, another had ordered his men not to contact him, and the third thought it was a Japanese trap. This resulted in the sailors having to spend four and a half days in the water among these aggressive sharks.

Kristine Phillips, writing for the *Washington Post,* penned an interview with a twenty-year-old marine from Kentucky by the name of Edgar Harrell. Harrell had just dropped off to sleep when the first explosion occurred. He was making his way to his commanding officer to get orders when he heard the ship's captain saying, "Abandon ship." He then made his way to the high side of the ship, grabbed a steel cable, "looked out into eternity," and jumped. He, along with others, spent several days in the water before being rescued.

At about noon on the fourth day after the explosion, Lieutenant Wilbur Gwinn was flying his bomber aircraft on a routine patrol when he looked down and spotted something in the water. Dropping down closer to investigate, he saw men aimlessly floating in the water. When he then radioed his base for help, Lieutenant Adrian Marks flew to the scene, dropping rafts and survival supplies as well as alerting the USS Doyle, the nearest ship. When Marks saw the men in the ocean being attack by sharks, he disobeyed orders not to land and placed his PBY plane in the twelve-foot swells of shark-infested waters. He began taxiing his plane to help the wounded and stragglers who were at the greatest risk. Since space in his plane was limited, Marks had his crew lash the survivors to the wings with parachute cords. As a result, he was able to rescue fifty-six survivors.

The Doyle arrived about midnight to rescue the remaining survivors from the water and the plane. After the rescue, sea conditions were not favorable for takeoff of the amphibious PBY-5A plane, and it was destroyed.

Charles B. McVay III, Captain of the USS Indianapolis, was court-martialed and convicted for failure to zigzag his ship, even though his orders were to zigzag at his discretion, weather permitting. He was never informed by the navy that Japanese submarines were operating in the area, even though the naval command knew the subs were active on the Indianapolis route to Leyte in the Philippines. The captain of the Japanese submarine testified at his military hearing that zigzagging would not have made any difference in the outcome of the sinking of the Indianapolis.

Fleet Admiral Chester Nimitz remitted McVay's sentence and restored him to active duty, from which he retired as a Rear Admiral in 1949. However, the hate mail he received from families who lost loved ones never stopped, and this apparently resulted in him taking his own life at age seventy in 1968.

In 1996, a sixth-grade student by the name of Hunter Scott began a research project on the Sinking of the Indianapolis. This eventually led to a congressional investigation. Then in October 2000, Congress passed a resolution that McVay's record should state that he was exonerated for the loss of the Indianapolis. President Bill Clinton signed the resolution.

The survivors of the USS Indianapolis have held reunions in Indianapolis since 1960. Seven out of the twenty living survivors attended in 2017. If the reunion continues in 2019, my goal is to attend. Reunions for my ship, the USS J. Franklin Bell, stopped with the twenty-first reunion in Tyler, Texas, in 2009. The reason was that our age made most of us physically unable to travel. I am one of the lucky ones, because I am writing this on a forty-nine-day cruise around South America. Well, I'm not just lucky; you would have to read my book *The Power of a Mother's Prayer* to know the real reason I am still very healthy.

At my retirement from the navy, fifty nations signed the United Nations Tablet to create the United Nations. Percy Spencer accidentally discovered that microwaves can heat food, and only about five thousand homes had television.

OTHER CONTRIBUTIONS TO VICTORY DURING WWII

It took more than just soldiers and sailors from the navy, army, and marines to win WWII. The next section deals with other warriors who were involved: US women, coast guards, submariners, and seabees.

> **They have given their sons to the military services. They have stoked the furnaces and hurried the factory wheels. They have made the planes and welded the tanks. Riveted the ships and rolled the shells.**
>
> **—President Franklin D. Roosevelt, addressing women's contributions to the war**

THE US WOMEN OF WORLD WAR II

Before the war, it was generally expected that a working man was the provider for his family. It was thought that any woman who took a job was taking it from a man who needed the job to support his family. However, with so many men away in the services, this approach could not continue. Women were recruited for jobs that were previously thought to be too physical: welding, machine repair, and operating tractors and other large machines. They also made uniforms, weapons, and ammunition plus tanks, planes, and trucks.

During World War II, 350,000 women served in the military, and sixteen were killed in combat. Sixty-seven were captured by the Japanese in 1942 and were held as POWs for two and a half years. During the early part of the WWII, all the branches of service established Women Auxiliary Corps. This included a group known as the Women Air Force Service Pilots (WASP), which was created in 1943 to ferry planes to stateside locations where male pilots were in short supply.

Recruitment of African Americans was limited to 10 percent to match the percentage of population in the US at that time. A total of 6,520 served during the war. Enlisted basic training was segregated for training, living, and dining.

Asian-Pacific American women first entered the military service during World War II. The army lowered the height and weight requirement for this group, and the unit was referred to as the Madame Chiang Kai-Shek Air WAC unit. They served in a variety of jobs, such as aerial photo interpretation, air traffic controllers, and weather forecasting.

More than fourteen thousand navy nurses served stateside, overseas on hospital ships, and as flight nurses during the war. Nursing could be a dangerous job during the war. As the Japanese closed in on Singapore in early 1942, sixty-five nurses were evacuated by ship. The Japanese sank the ship they were on, and twelve nurses were lost by drowning. Another group of twenty-two nurses were captured by the Japanese on the Indonesian Island of Banka. They were marched to the waterfront and executed by machine gun fire.

In 1942, the director of the Women's Bureau, Mary Anderson, reported that about 2,800,000 women were engaged in war work, and the number was expected to double by the end of that year. When including all the services, such as Office of Strategic Services, the American Red Cross, and the United Service Organizations, plus the Rosie the Riveters in factories and including transportation, agricultural, and office work, nearly nineteen million women supported the war effort.

It was interesting to read Denise Kiernan's *The Girls of Atomic City*. It is almost unimaginable that these young girls in their late teens and early twenties could be trusted to not talk about what they were doing. They were not only restricted from talking to outsiders, but to each other as well. It just had to come from a deep and sincere devotion to serving their country and the willingness to support the overall war effort to the maximum extent.

There are numerous women who deserved to be listed as forgotten warriors. But one stands out in my mind as I researched American women of World War II for my book. Ruby Bradley was a career nurse who was serving as a hospital administrator on the island of Luzon in the Philippines when the Japanese arrived in early 1942. She and another nurse, along with a doctor, chose to hide out in the hills after the takeover by the Japanese. They were turned over to the Japanese by the locals and sent back to their camp, which had become a prisoner camp. They once again went to work, attending the sick and injured with little supply of medicines or equipment. She spent more than three years in this camp trying to comfort the sick and dying. When finally freed, she had lost weight— from 110 pounds down to eighty-four.

After the war, she earned her bachelor's degree. Then, in 1950, she went to Korea as the 8th Army Chief Nurse. Working at the front lines, she was the last to leave by plane, as her ambulance was destroyed by enemy shelling as she departed. During her career, she was awarded thirty-four medals and citations (which included two Legions of Merit and two Bronze Stars) and promoted to Army Colonel. She was also awarded the Florence Nightingale Medal by the International Red Cross, which is their highest award.

World War II changed the lives of most women, and the process is continuing today with a constant fight for equal pay, promotions, and opportunities. I would guess that it is fair to say the genie is out of the bottle.

THE UNITED STATES SUBMARINE SERVICE

In the year 2000, the US celebrated its first century with the development of the submarine, which became important to the winning of World War II. Through a design competition, the navy gave John Holland the contract to build the first submarine, the Plunger. Then in 1900, John Holland again won the competition to build the sixty-four-ton vessel at a cost of $160,000, which was named the USS Holland, or SS-1. It was commissioned on October 12, 1900. Initially, the engines were run on gasoline, but due to the volatility of gas, they were soon switched to diesel engines.

During World War II, the submarine services had the highest casualty percentage of all the armed services. Fifty-two submarines were lost during this period. Some sixteen thousand personnel served on submarines during the war, of which 375 officers and 3,131 enlisted men were killed.

During World War II, the submarine force comprised only about 2 percent of the US Navy but sank more than thirty percent of the Japanese Navy. They also strangled the Japanese economy by sinking almost five million tons of badly needed imports of material needed for the war effort.

World War II submarines were basically surface ships that could travel a limited time underwater. The engines, which were diesel, gave high surface speed and long range. But the speed and range under water was greatly reduced with the electric motors, which were powered by batteries. Recharging the batteries meant surfacing to run the air breathing diesels, and this was required about 90 percent of the time, even on combat patrols.

The USS Balao, which was commissioned in February 1943, carried a crew of ten officers and seventy enlisted men. It was 312 feet long and carried twenty-four torpedoes and was equipped with deck guns. The Balao had a surface speed of more than twenty miles per hour, which was cut in half when submerged. If the underwater speed was reduced to two knots per hour, she could stay submerged for forty-eight hours.

The submarine service played a significant role in the defeat of Japan—not only in sinking ships, but also in penetrating hostile areas (for picking up aviators who had been shot down by the enemy), extracting coastwatchers or moving them to different areas, doing reconnaissance for potential invasion sites, and many other activities associated with fighting a war that need covert action.

It was either a stroke of luck or divine intervention that the Japanese commanders who brought destruction to Pearl Harbor ignored the subbase. They elected to bypass the submarine base, which allowed the US to keep its most effective warship, the submarine, active in the early stages of WWII. It was the submarine force that carried the load in those early years of the war so that the industrial might of the US could spring into action.

MacArthur saw the value of the submarine in the delivery of personnel and supplies at Corregidor. He used the submarine for more special missions than any other commander. This did not sit well with some of the submarine commanders, as they felt their mission was to seek and destroy Japanese shipping. However, the experience submarine crews gained while performing special missions paid huge dividends in the guerrilla and resistance operations throughout the South Pacific.

I have great admiration for the sailors who served in our submarine fleet. The thought of having to talk in whispers and walk in stocking feet when in enemy waters to avoid a noise that could be detected by the enemy would be hard to comply with. And then, the bone-chilling explosions of nearby depth charges while submerged in enemy waters required courage and bravery of a special breed. This special breed is illustrated by an event in enemy waters just off the coast of Japan for Sergeant Richard Heuver. He was a tail gunner in a B-29 bomber that had lost all but one engine during a bombing raid over Japan. His story is about how the Submarine Service saved his life and that of his crewmates because their plane had to be ditched.

> A "buddy" Support crew guided the troubled crew over a pickup area and the troubled crew bailed out, landing in about a mile-wide area. The last crew member jumped at an elevation of only 800 feet above the water. Within 45 minutes all crew members of the plane were in the submarine.

I provide another real-life illustration of how engaged the submarine service was during WWII. The less than 2 percent of sailors who served in the navy sank a total of 214 Japanese ships. These included four large aircraft carriers, four small aircraft carriers, one battleship, three heavy cruisers, eight light cruisers, forty-three destroyers, twenty-three large submarines, and 1,178 merchant ships. These numbers represented more than 55 percent of all Japanese ships. This fact means that the Submarine Service did more than all the others combined, which included navy surface forces, navy air forces, and US Army Air Corps combined.

Fleet Admiral Chester W. Nimitz had this to say after the war was over: "We who survived World War II and were privileged to rejoin our loved ones at home, salute those gallant officers and men of our submarines who lost their lives in that long struggle. We shall never forget that it was our submarines that held the lines against the enemy while our fleets replaced losses and repaired wounds."

Our wholehearted thanks should go to all submariners and the pilots who fought at Midway as well as the troops who conquered the jungles of the Solomon Islands. They should never be put into the category of forgotten warriors.

THE UNITED STATES COAST GUARD SERVICE

Another group that should not be forgotten is our coast guard. All too often, this group is thought to be a military agency that protects the US borders from outsiders. Nothing could be further from the truth. The coast guard played a major role in the march across the Pacific. At the same time, they did patrol the coast of the US. Seaman 2nd Class John Cullen received the Legion of Merit for catching the German sabotage team that tried to enter the US at Amagansett, New York, on June 13, 1942.

The coast guard on duty in the Pacific theater (Courtesy of Military Archives, public domain)

The history of the United States Coast Guard goes back to the United States Revenue Service, which was created on August 4, 1790, as part of the Department of Treasury. The Revenue Cutter Service and the United States Life-Saving Service was merged to become the Coast Guard.

The law stated that the coast guard as established on January 28, 1915, will always be a military service and a branch of the armed forces. Then in 2006, a law was passed that stated, "In case of war, and upon the direction of Congress, or the President directs, the Coast Guard shall operate as a service under the Department of the Navy."

I personally became acquainted with the coast guard during the invasion of Tinian in the Mariana Islands. I, along with all the others of our beach party for this invasion, were transferred to the coast guard ship the USS Cavalier (APA 37) because our ship the Bell was going to be part of the fake landing on the south of Tinian. We of the J. Franklin Bell beach party had to go with the actual landing on the northwest side of the island.

The coast guard USS Cavalier (APA-37) (Courtesy of Military Archives, public domain)

The Cavalier was also in our convoy for the invasion of Leyte, and it was here in the Philippines that she was torpedoed a little later, which resulted in injury to fifty shipmates and damage to the extent that she had to be towed for repairs. But she went on to serve in the Korean and Vietnam wars.

The coast guard had under its command during World War II numerous ships. For example, it had twenty-two troopships, twenty amphibious cargo ships, nine attack transports (APA's), and thirty Edsall Class Destroyer Escorts, to mention a few. The Edsall Class Destroyer Escort was used primarily for convoy escorts duty in the Atlantic.

The only coast guardsman to receive the Medal of Honor was Signalman 1st Class Douglas Munro, who earned his award as small boat coxswain during the battle of Guadalcanal in 1942. (See his citation in the Battle of Guadalcanal section.)

Several Hollywood movie stars became sailors in the coast guard: Gig Young, Cesar Romero, and Richard Cromwell. They all served in different capacities in the Pacific for several years. During WWII, 214,239 persons served in the coast guard. That number included 12,846 women. The coast guard lost a total of 1,917 personnel, with 574 losing their lives in action.

On January 29, 1945, the USS Serpens (AK-97), a coast guard-manned liberty ship, exploded off Guadalcanal in the Solomon Islands while loading depth charges. This was the biggest single loss of the war for the coast guard, which included 193 coast guardsmen, fifty-six army stevedores, and one US Public Health Service officer.

THE UNITED STATES NAVAL CONSTRUCTION BATTALIONS "SEABEES"

In the late 1930s, it became evident that the US was not far from being involved in the war in Europe. With this concern, Congress authorized the expansion of naval shore activities. The result was construction projects initiated in the Caribbean and the central Pacific. At that time, it was navy policy to award the construction to civilian contractors who employed locals as well as American civilians.

Under international law, civilians were encouraged not to resist enemy military attacks. Resistance meant the employees could be executed as guerrillas. Therefore, the need for a militarized naval construction force was obvious.

Rear Admiral Ben Morrell became Chief of the Bureau of Yards and Docks in 1937. This office oversees the Civil Engineer Corps. On December 28, 1941, he requested specific authority to develop the Naval Construction Force. He received authority to do so on January 5, 1942.

The average age of the men being enlisted was thirty-seven, and the seabees were officially named on March 5, 1942. A problem developed immediately over who should command the construction battalions. The Bureau of Naval Personnel objected to the command being given to the Civil Engineer Corps, but Admiral Morrell personally presented this question to the Secretary of the Navy. On March 19, 1942, the secretary gave authority to the Civil Engineer Corps. It has been said that Admiral Morrell's success in achieving this contributed greatly to the success and fame of the seabees.

The name of the seabees was created by Frank J. Infrate, who was working as a file clerk at the Naval Air Station, Quonset, Rhode Island. He was known for drawing caricatures of the men in his area. A navy lieutenant asked him to draw a Disney-type insignia that would identify and represent this new battalion. After considerable thought, he concluded that the bee would be appropriate. His reasons were

1. "Busy as a bee" was a noted phrase, and bees would not hurt people unless they were bothered first.
2. He gave the bee a Tommy gun to illustrate its fierce nature.
3. He added the C. E. C. insignia for Civil Engineer Corps.
4. He encircled the logo with a Q for Quonset.

The next day, the logo was sent off to Admiral Morrell, and the only change was switching the Q with a rope, which Admiral Morrell felt tied it to the navy. During World War II, the seabees worked in both the Atlantic and Pacific Theaters of war. At a cost of $11 billion and many casualties, they constructed more than four hundred advanced bases. In the Pacific, this was along three figurative roads: the north Pacific road through the Aleutians; the central Pacific road through Hawaiian, Marshall, Gilbert, Mariana, and Ryukyu islands; and the south Pacific road through the South Sea Islands to Samoa, the Solomons', New Guinea, and the Philippines. All the roads converged on Japan.

Along these three roads, the seabees constructed 111 major airstrips, 441 piers, 2,558 ammunition magazines, seven hundred square blocks of warehouses, hospitals to serve seventy thousand patients, tanks for the storage of one hundred million gallons of gasoline, and housing to serve 1,500,000 men.

All the above accomplishments were not easy, as the seabees suffered more than two hundred combat deaths and earned more than two thousand Purple Hearts. They were active on four continents and served on more than three hundred islands.

Their first major activity was setting up bases in the Aleutian chain of islands with a base at Adak to serve the troops for the battles of Attu and Kiska. Although the US never pushed in this direction toward Japan, the bases built by the seabees kept the Japanese looking over their shoulders for fear of an attack from that direction.

The road through south and southwest Pacific had to go through the steaming jungles toward the Philippines, and their first stop was the Society Islands. The seabees landed on an island in this group called Bora Bora. The code name given to this island for military purpose was BOBCAT. So, the seabees called themselves the bobcats. They were the advanced party of more than 325,000 men who served in the naval construction force during World War II.

I recently had the opportunity to see some of the gun emplacements on these islands and had to say to myself, "It is not possible to get the guns up here and build the concrete foundations that they sat on at these peaks." But there they were, defying all logic, thanks to the bobcats.

The purpose of the seabees landing on these islands was to build a fueling station that would fuel the ships and planes necessary to keep the shipping lanes open to Australia. After landing on what seemed like a tropical paradise, the bobcats discovered that they had to deal with continual rainfall, fifty varieties of dysentery, skin disease, and the dreaded elephantiasis.

The island of Espiritu Santo in the New Hebrides was the closest in proximity to the Japanese-held Guadalcanal. The need to destroy the Japanese airfield nearing completion on Guadalcanal was imperative. But to do this, an airfield was needed on Espiritu Santo for US planes. Within an incredible twenty days, the seabees had carved out a six thousand-foot airstrip in a virgin jungle. As a result of this effort, the US was able to destroy the Japanese airbase. Then when the marines landed on Guadalcanal, the seabees followed them ashore and became the first seabees to build under combat conditions. The seabees then began repairing the airfield that their effort had just permitted the US to destroy. The airfield was Henderson Field, which the Japanese tried many times to retake but were repulsed on every attempt. The airfield was named after the marine pilot lost at Midway.

They had to work continuously, because the Japanese kept bombing the airstrip, but the seabees managed to keep it open, which was critical to the success of the Guadalcanal invasion. It was here that the first decorated hero of the seabees was named: Seaman 2nd Class Lawrence C. "Bucky" Meyer USNR. He had salvaged an abandoned machine gun and used it to shoot down a Japanese zero that was strafing his area. He was awarded the Silver Star posthumously, because he was killed thirteen days later when Japanese naval gunfire hit a gasoline barge on which he was working.

Another act of heroism occurred on the landing on Treasury Island in the Solomons'. Fireman 1st Class Aurelio Tassone USNR was driving his bulldozer ashore when he was told by Lieutenant Turnbull that a Japanese pillbox was holding up their advance. Tassone drove his dozer toward the pillbox with the blade up as a shield while the Lieutenant provided cover fire with his carbine. The result was that all twelve occupants of the pillbox were killed. For this, Tassone received the Silver Star.

The seabees were only expected to fight to defend what they had built, but throughout World War II, the seabees were awarded thirty-three Silver Stars and five Navy Crosses. Their losses during the war were 272 enlisted men and eighteen officers killed in action. An additional five hundred seabees died of construction accidents.

The seabees continued their march across the Pacific, often landing with the invasion force and setting up construction projects within hours after H-hour on D-day. This was common for Tarawa in the Gilberts, Kwajalein, Eniwetok, and Majuro in the Marshalls and in the Marianas at Saipan, Tinian, Guam, and Okinawa.

When you stop for a moment and think about all the troops, ships, and aircraft in the Pacific and Atlantic Theaters of war having to be maintained and supplied with provisions to keep them in fighting shape, then you can realize how important the seabees were to wining World War II.

MEDAL FF HONOR HEROES OF THE PACIFIC NOT INCLUDED IN ANY OF THE ABOVE BATTLES

For a detailed description and original citation for those not shown here, please go to *www.themedalofhonor.org*.

Richard Nott Antrim, born December 17, 1907, in Peru, Indiana. Acting instantly on behalf of a naval officer who was subjected to a vicious clubbing by a frenzied Japanese guard venting his insane wrath upon the helpless prisoner, Comdr. (then Lt.) Antrim boldly intervened, attempting to quiet the guard and finally persuading him to discuss the charges against the officer. With the entire Japanese force assembled and making extraordinary preparations for the threatened beating and with the tension heightened by 2,700 Allied prisoners rapidly closing in, Comdr. Antrim courageously appealed to the fanatic enemy, risking his own life in a desperate effort to mitigate the punishment. When the other had been beaten unconscious by fifteen blows of a hawser and was repeatedly kicked by three soldiers to a point beyond which he could not survive, Comdr. Antrim gallantly stepped forward and indicated to the perplexed guards that he would take the remainder of the punishment, throwing the Japanese completely off balance in their amazement and eliciting a roar of acclaim from the suddenly inspired Allied prisoners. By his fearless leadership and valiant concern for the welfare of another, he not only saved the life of a fellow officer and stunned the Japanese into sparing his own life, but also brought about a new respect for

American officers and men and a great improvement in camp living conditions.

John Duncan Bulkeley, born August 19, 1911, in New York, New York

George Ham Cannon, born November 5, 1915, in Webster Groves, Missouri

Horace S. Carswell Jr. piloted a B-bomber in a one-plane strike against a Japanese convoy in the South China Sea on the night of October 26, 1944. Taking the enemy force of twelve ships escorted by at least two destroyers by surprise, he made one bombing run at six hundred feet, scoring a near miss on one warship and escaping without drawing fire. He circled, and fully realizing that the convoy was thoroughly alerted and would meet his next attack with a barrage of antiaircraft fire, he began a second low-level run that culminated in two direct hits on a large tanker. A hail of steel from Japanese guns riddled the bomber, knocking out two engines, damaging a third, crippling the hydraulic system, puncturing one gasoline tank, ripping uncounted holes in the aircraft, and wounding the copilot; but by magnificent display of flying skill, Maj. Carswell controlled the plane's plunge toward the sea and carefully forced it into a halting climb in the direction of the China shore. On reaching land, where it would have been possible to abandon the staggering bomber, one of the crew discovered that his parachute had been ripped by flak and rendered useless; the pilot, hoping to cross mountainous terrain and reach a base, continued onward until the third engine failed. He ordered the crew to bail out while he struggled to maintain altitude and, refusing to save himself, chose to remain with his comrade and attempt a crash landing. He died when the airplane struck a mountainside and burned. With consummate gallantry and intrepidity, Maj. Carswell gave his life in a supreme effort to save all members of his crew.

Henry Talmage Elrod, born September 27, 1905, in Rebecca, Georgia

Ernest Edwin Evans, born August 13, 1908, in Pawnee, Oklahoma

Eugene Bennett Fluckey was commanding officer of the DSS Barb during her eleventh war patrol along the east coast of China from December 19, 1944, to February 15, 1945. After sinking a large enemy ammunition ship and damaging additional tonnage during a running two-hour night battle on January 8, Comdr. Fluckey, in an exceptional feat of brilliant deduction and bold tracking on January 25, located a concentration of more than thirty enemy ships in the lower reaches of Nankuan Chiang (Mamkwan Harbor). Fully aware that a safe retirement would necessitate an hour's run at full speed through the untitled, mined, and rock-obstructed waters, he bravely ordered, "Battle station—torpedoes!" In a daring penetration of the heavy enemy screen and riding in five fathoms (nine meters) of water, he launched the *Barb's* last forward torpedoes at a three thousand-yard (2.7 kilometer) range. Quickly bringing the ship's stem tubes to bear, he turned loose four more torpedoes into the enemy, obtaining eight direct hits on six of the main targets to explode a large ammunition ship and cause inestimable damage by the resultant flying shells and other pyrotechnics. Clearing the treacherous area at high speed, he brought the Barb through to safety, and four days later, he sank a large Japanese freighter to complete a record of heroic combat achievement.

Donald Arthur Gary, born July 23, 1903, in Findlay, Ohio
Nathan Green Gordon, born September 4, 1916, in Morrilton, Alaska
Owen Francis Patrick Hammerberg, born May 31, 1920, in Daggett, Michigan
Joe P. Martinez, born (date of birth unknown) in Taos, New Mexico
Martin O. May, born April 18, 1922, in Philipsburg, New Jersey
David McCampbell, born January 16, 1910, in Bessemer, Alabama

Joseph Timothy O'Callahan, born May 14, 1904, in Boston, Massachusetts. O'Callahan was chaplain on board the USS *Franklin* when that vessel was fiercely attacked by enemy Japanese aircraft during offensive operations near Kobe, Japan, on March 19, 1945. A valiant and forceful leader, calmly braving the perilous barriers of flame and twisted metal to aid his men and his ship, Lt. Comdr. O'Callahan groped his way through smoke-filled corridors to the open flight deck and into the midst of violently exploding bombs, shells, rockets, and other armament. With the ship rocked by incessant explosions, with debris and fragments raining down and fires raging in ever-increasing fury, he ministered to the wounded and dying, comforting and encouraging men of all faiths. He organized and led firefighting crews into the blazing inferno on the flight deck; he directed the jettisoning of live ammunition and the flooding of the magazine. He manned a hose to cool hot, armed bombs rolling dangerously on the listing deck, continuing his efforts, despite searing, suffocating smoke that forced men to fall back gasping and imperiled others who replaced them. Serving with courage, fortitude, and deep spiritual strength, Lt. Comdr. O'Callahan inspired the gallant officers and men of the Franklin to fight heroically and with profound faith in the face of almost certain death and to return their stricken ship to port.

Edward Henry O'Hare, born March 13, 1914, in St. Louis, Missouri

Oscar Verner Peterson, born August 27, 1899, in Prentice, Wisconsin

Authur Murray Preston, born November 1, 1913, in Washington, District of Columbia

Albert Harold Rooks, born December 29, 1891, in Colton, Washington

Clyde Thomason, born May 23, 1914, in Atlanta, Georgia

George Watson, born in Birmingham, Alabama

THE ACE FIGHTER PILOTS

The following is a group of pilots who fought air battles all over the Pacific campaign during World War II. They were not associated with individual campaigns. But as individuals, they were heroes in every respect. For their actions in battle, they were awarded the Medal of Honor.

Gregory Boyington was in action against enemy Japanese forces in Central Solomons' area from September 12, 1943, to January 3, 1944. Consistently outnumbered throughout successive hazardous flights over heavily defended hostile territory, Major Byington struck at the enemy with daring and courageous persistence, leading his squadron into combat with devastating results to Japanese shipping, shore installations, and aerial forces. Resolute in his efforts to inflict crippling damage on the enemy, Major Byington led a formation of twenty-four fighters over Kahili on October 17, and persistently circling the airdrome where sixty hostile aircraft were grounded, he boldly challenged the Japanese to send up planes. Under his brilliant command, our fighters shot down twenty enemy craft in the ensuing action without the loss of a single ship. A superb airman and determined fighter against overwhelming odds, Major Boyington personally destroyed twenty-six of the many Japanese planes shot down by his squadron and by his forceful leadership developed the combat readiness in his command that was a distinctive factor in the allied aerial achievements in this vitally strategic area.

Jefferson J. DeBlanc, during aerial operations against enemy Japanese forces off Kolombangara Island in the Solomons group on January 31, 1943. Taking off with his section as escort for a strike force of dive bombers and torpedo planes ordered to attack Japanese surface vessels, First Lieutenant DeBlanc led his flight directly to the target area where, at fourteen thousand feet, our strike force encountered a large number of Japanese zeros protecting the enemy's surface craft. In company with the other fighters, First Lieutenant DeBlanc instantly engaged the hostile planes and aggressively interred their repeated attempts to drive off our bombers, persevering in his efforts to protect the diving planes and waging fierce combat until, picking up a call for assistance from the dive bombers under attack by enemy float planes at one thousand feet, he broke off his engagement with the zeros, plunged into the formation of float planes, and disrupted the savage attack, enabling our dive bombers and torpedo planes to complete their runs on the Japanese surface disposition and to withdraw without further incident. Although his escort mission was fulfilled upon the safe retirement of the bombers, First Lieutenant DeBlanc courageously remained on the scene despite a rapidly diminishing fuel supply and, boldly challenging the enemy's superior number of float planes, fought a valiant battle against terrific odds, seizing the tactical advantage and striking repeatedly to destroy three of the hostile aircraft and to disperse the remainder. Prepared to maneuver his damaged plane back to base, he had climbed aloft and set his course when he discovered two zeros closing in behind. Undaunted, he opened fire and blasted both zeros from the sky in short, bitterly fought action that resulted in such hopeless damage to his plane that he was forced to bail out at a perilously low altitude atop the trees on enemy-held Kolombangara.

Thomas Buchanan McGuire Jr., born August 1, 1920, in Ridgewood, New Jersey. After service in the United States and Alaska, he was ordered in March 1943 to the 49th Fighter Group of the 5th United States Air Force, then operating in the southwest Pacific Area, providing an early air screen for Darwin and northern Australia. Subsequently, he was transferred to the 475th Fighter Group, 13th Air Force, where he won promotion to Major. He was already a leading ace with a record of thirty-one Japanese planes shot down when he volunteered on December 5, 1944, to lead a squadron of P-38s on a bomber escort mission over Mabalacar Airdrome on Luzon, Philippines. He shot down three of twenty Japanese zero fighters that attacked his squadron. The next day, on a similar mission over Clark Field, near Manila, he exposed himself in order to draw fire away from a crippled bomber and shot down three of the four fighters that were attacking it. Another score on his way home that day brought his total to thirty-eight. On January 7, 1945, while leading a flight of four P-38s over Los Negros Island, he attempted a highly dangerous maneuver in order to aid a comrade who was losing an encounter with a Japanese zero and crashed. He was posthumously awarded the Medal of Honor in March 1946 for his actions on December 25–26, 1944, and January 7, 1945. His score of thirty-eight enemy kills made him the second leading American fighter pilot of World War II, following Major Richard Bong.

James Swett, in a daring flight to intercept a wave of 150 Japanese planes. First Lieutenant Swett unhesitatingly hurled his four-plane division into action against a formation of fifteen enemy bombers, and during his dive, he personally exploded three hostile planes in midair with accurate and deadly fire. Although separated from his division while clearing the heavy concentration of anti-aircraft fire, he boldly attacked six enemy bombers, engaged the first four in turn, and unaided, shot them down in flames. Exhausting his ammunition as he closed the fifth Japanese bomber, he relentlessly drove his attack against terrific opposition that partially disabled his engine, shattered the windscreen, and slashed his face. Despite this, he brought his battered plane down with skillful precision in the water off Tulagi without further injury. Superb airmanship and tenacious fighting spirit enabled First Lieutenant Swett to destroy eight enemy bombers in a single flight.

Kenneth A. Walsh, born on November 24, 1916, in Brooklyn, New York. Walsh was a pilot in Marine Fighting Squadron 124 in aerial combat against enemy Japanese forces in the Solomon Islands area. Determined to thwart the enemy's attempt to bomb Allied ground forces and shipping at Vella Lavella on August 15, 1943, 1st Lt. Walsh repeatedly dived his plane into an enemy formation outnumbering his own division six to one, and although his plane was hit numerous times, he shot down two Japanese dive bombers and one fighter. After developing engine trouble on August 30 during a vital escort mission, 1st Lt. Walsh landed his mechanically disabled plane at Munda, quickly replaced it with another, and proceeded to rejoin his flight over Kahili. Separated from his escort group when he encountered approximately fifty Japanese zeros, he unhesitatingly attacked, striking with relentless fury in his lone battle against a powerful force. He destroyed four hostile fighters before cannon shellfire forced him to make a dead stick landing off Vella Lavella, where he was later picked up.

Another poem, "Tribute to the WWII Generation" by Timothy Churchill, applies to all those all who served in World War II at home or abroad and in every branch of service.

Tribute to the WWII Generation

A generation, tapped by fate,
To bear the nation's pain,
Was destined to become the core,
Of courage, loss, and gain,

A generation born to strife,
Whose time was fraught with fear,
With drought and dust across the land,
And stark depression near

The hardships brought on fortitude,
To guard our "freedom" star,
American courage, faced the test,
To fight a worldwide war.

Our nation's very heart was sore;
We faced our "longest day,"
Defend our shores, our liberty,
Or die along the way

That generation gained its strength
Through brotherhood, and pride,
With love of country, patriots came,
Five hundred thousand died

With gratitude and honor due,
For all they lost, and gave,
A generation making safe,
Our own "home of the brave

The next sections describe some
interesting facts about WWII.

SOME INTERESTING FACTS ABOUT WORLD WAR II

Even though it's out of context with what I am writing, I must mention something that happened on the other side of the world during WWII. My brother Norman was awarded the Bronze Star for bravery in action in the European Theater of war. The citation reads as follows.

> Norman L. Young 35 675 468 Private, Calvary Troop "C", 93rd Cavalry Reconnaissance Squadron, Mechanized, for meritorious achievement in connection with military operations against an enemy of the United States on April 17, 1945 near Mettmann, Germany. Private Young, Radio electrician, voluntarily exposed himself to enemy fire to drive his one-quarter ton truck up and down the column, disseminating vital information to the various platoons. Through his coolness under fire and initiative the unit commander was able to maintain constant contact with his men despite the failure of radio. His exemplary conduct is worthy of the highest praise. He entered military service from Danville, Kentucky in 1942.

> Signed John Milikin
> Major General US Army
> Commanding

Norman passed away on April 6, 2015.

The Enola Gay became well known for dropping the first atomic bomb on Hiroshima. Few people know the name of the plane that dropped the bomb on Nagasaki. The name was Bock's Car after the plane's commander, Frederick Bock. Enola Gay was the name of the mother of Paul Tibbets, the pilot.

Atomic bomb explosion over Hiroshima
(Courtesy of US Navy, public domain)

The bomb will never go off, and I
speak as an expert in explosives.
—Admiral William D. Leahy (advising President
Truman on the atom bomb project, 1945)

After dropping the bomb on Hiroshima, which exploded at 1,890 feet above ground, the plane *Enola Gay* raced away after making a 180-degree turn to maximize the distance between the plane and the bomb. But the shockwave from the explosion caught up with the plane and shook the plane like a near miss from flak. The mushroom cloud boiled up to 45,000 feet high and was still rising. The city below had disappeared under a blanket of smoke and fire.

During World War II, the Japanese launched nine thousand wind ship weapons of paper and rubberized-silk balloons that carried incendiary and anti-personnel bombs to the US. More than one thousand balloons hit their target, and they reached as far east as Michigan. Only six American deaths resulted from a balloon bomb. These included five children and a pregnant woman on a picnic in Oregon.

The Japanese kamikaze (divine wind) tactic was suggested on October 19, 1944, by Vice-Admiral Onishi to balance the technological advantage of the invading American forces. Through the numbers are disputed, approximately 2,800 kamikaze pilots died. They sunk thirty-four US ships, damaged 368, killed 4,900 sailors, and wounded ten thousand.

World War II was the most destructive conflict in history. It cost more money, damaged more property, killed more people, and caused more far-reaching changes than any other war in history.

At the time of the Pearl Harbor attack, there were ninety-six ships anchored in the harbor. During the attack, eighteen were sunk or seriously damaged, including eight battleships. Three hundred fifty aircraft were destroyed or damaged.

The United States Air Force, a part of the army during World War II, became a separate branch of the military after the World War II.

A private in 1941 earned $21 per month; pay increased to $50 per month in 1942.

During World War II, 650,000 jeeps were built. American factories also produced three hundred thousand military aircraft, 89,000 tanks, three million machine guns, and seven million rifles.

If it had become necessary to drop the third atom bomb on Japan, the city that would have been hit was Tokyo.

During World War I, Japan fought on the side of Britain, France, and the US and felt cheated by its failure to gain much territory when the peace treaty was composed. Additionally, in the 1920s, the Japanese government came under the control of fanatical nationalists and eventually sided with the Germans.

Author Ian Fleming based his character 007 on the Yugoslavian-born spy Dusko Popov. Popov spoke at least five languages and came up with his own formula for invisible ink. He obtained information that the Japanese were planning an air strike on Pearl Harbor, but the FBI did not act on his warning. Popov later lived in the US in a penthouse and created a reputation as a playboy. He wrote an account of his activities in his novel *Spy, Counterspy* in 1974.

From 1942, the marines in the Pacific used the Navajo language as their secret code. Around four hundred Navajo Indians were trained to use the code. The Japanese never cracked the code.

The next sections show in table form the numbers of casualties by country and type.

TOTAL WORLD WAR II PACIFIC THEATER CASUALTIES

Asia and the Pacific Theater of War by Country (Killed/Wounded)

Table 20 below is a summary of the major players in the Pacific Theater of war and indicates the nearly three to one ratio for the US in wounded to kill and the opposite of nearly eighteen to one for the Japanese for the kill to wounded.

Killed/Missing	Wounded/POW
(1) 111,606	(1) 274,722
(2) 1,740,000	(2) 135,440
(3) 4,000,000	(3) 7,000,000*
(4) 9,470	(4) 35,723

*China also had an approximate 18,000,000 Civilians death

1: USA, 2: Japan, 3: China, 4: Australia

WWII Casualties by Nation

Table 21 is a summary of death and casualties by the major Allied countries in World War II. I am convinced that our higher ratio of wounded to killed is the result of our better application of medical support on the battlefield. A big thanks to our army medics and navy corpsmen.

Deaths	Wounded
(1) 291,557	(1) 670,846
(2) 6,115,000	(2) 14,013,000
(3) 42,042	(3) 53,145
(4) 357,116	(4) 369,267

Rows 1 US, 2 USSR, 3 Canada, 4 United Kingdom

TOTAL ALLIED CASUALTIES FOR WORLD WAR II OF ALL COUNTRIES

Table 22 is the casualties of World War II in deaths and wounded all over the world.

Battle Deaths	20,858,000
Wounded	27,372,900
Civilian Deaths	59,487,000

Total Estimated Casualties for all Counties Somewhere Between 96 Million to 108 Million

The next section describes four of the many reunions held by the shipmates of the USS J. Franklin Bell.

SHIPMATE REUNIONS—COMMENTARY ON FIVE REUNIONS WITH POETRY BY TIMOTHY CHURCHILL

CANTON, OHIO (1997)

After my first retirement in 1985, I searched each year to discover if my ship, USS J. Franklin Bell, was having a reunion. Finally, I wrote to the navy in Washington, DC and received a prompt response with a contact for the tenth reunion in Canton, Ohio. It was really exciting to meet shipmates like Chet Maki, Bob Tagatz, Tim Churchill, Doug Webb, and best of all, Naval Officer Melvin Badger, who was the officer in charge of the beach party on Saipan and Tinian. It was just great to talk to all the shipmates but especially Lt. Badger, because we rehashed our time on the beach during the invasions. He told me that he had recommended all the beach party for the Silver Star for what we went through on Saipan and Tinian, but it was turned down. I only missed a couple reunions during the next eleven years, and that was because my wife became ill with Alzheimer's. But I was able to host two more reunions in Kentucky during the period she was ill.

LEXINGTON, KENTUCKY (2005)

The reunion in 2005 was staged at the Campbell House in Lexington, Kentucky and included a day at the races (Keeneland), a bus tour to a horse farm, dinner at Boone Tavern in Berea, and a pig roast at my farm. This was the second of three such reunions I hosted over the years.

The Bluegrass Land Again

Once more in old Kentucky,
The horse and bluegrass state,
Where The Bell crew got together,
Before time gets too late.

In the year two, aught, aught, five,
On Ralph Young's orchard farm,
The pig roast brought us running,
And the sunshine made us warm.

We lived again the olden days,
Young sailors brave, and bold,
We fought and won the World War Two,
Our normal lives on "hold."

We scattered to the four winds then,
Each going his own way,
But once each year, the faithful few,
Join up to cheer the day.

We reminisce, and honor those,
Who sailed on to distant seas,
They were men who shared our world,
Our "shipmates," if you please.

So, some are gone, and some remain,
But we shall meet once more,
If not on land we fought to save,
Then on some "other" shore.

Tim Churchill told me that he got on the wrong elevator in Denver, Colorado after his discharge from the navy and accidentally ended up in an army recruiting office, where he negotiated a commission as an army officer and was shipped to Germany, where met and fell in love with Helga, who has been his wife ever since. Helga is a beautiful lady, and they make a great pair.

GOLD CANYON, ARIZONA (2007)

One of the most enjoyable reunions was in 2007 with Max and Marlene Miller in Arizona. It was built around their beautiful and spacious home and took in about all the sights in the area, which Tim describes in his poem. I remember it well, because it was a stopover for Janice and me on our three-month honeymoon trip to Thailand, China, and other areas in southeast Asia.

Thanks for the Memories ©

"Thanks for the Memories"
From "shipmates," friends, and wives;
From sons and daughters of the crew,
You've enriched all our lives.

You hosted our reunion there,
In Arizona land,
And gave us memories to last,
Until the last command.

We will remember moonlit nights,
And trips to outer scenes,
And all the camaraderie
With what that really means.

Our trips along Apache Trail,
Saguaro Lake so blue,
The "Rockin' R" with western swing,
No end of things to do.

As we salute J. Franklin Bell,
With reverent thoughts of those,
Who served with us in World War Two,
Now resting in repose.

As World War Two vets fade away,
From many to so few,
Then those of us, who yet survive,
Can meet, as comrades do.

And somewhere past the great beyond,
When Bos'n sounds his call,
We muster on the Quarter Deck,
To answer, one and all.

REUNION IN DANVILLE, KENTUCKY IN 2008

Timothy Churchill almost always had a reason for his poetry. It could be written after a close call in combat, a Veterans Day parade when the organizers of parade would request a poem, or a USS J. Franklin Bell reunion.

To understand the meaning of many, you would have to know some of the events that occurred. For example, in his poem "Reunion in Danville," you must know that shipmate Tom Lyons, who owned a travel business in Texas, flew into Louisville rather than Lexington, where I was waiting to pick up him and his daughter Joy for the trip to our reunion headquarters in Danville, Kentucky. I was waiting at the American Airlines baggage carousel when my cell phone rang, and it was Tom on the phone, saying, "Where are you, Ralph Young?"

I said, "Waiting for you at the American Airlines baggage."

Tom said, "That is impossible, because I am at American Airline, and you are nowhere in sight." When asked what airport he was in, his answer was, "Louisville."

I said, "Wait right there, Tom. I will see you in about ninety minutes."

Another part of the poem relates to the fact that shipmate Bob Tagatz was without a doubt the luckiest guy at all our reunions. (In my ninety-four years here on earth, I have also noticed that the luckiest people always seem to be the most talented.) Whether gambling at the casinos or playing raffles, he seemed to always win. So, when it came to horse racing, none of us could keep up with shipmate Tony Tralla. Tim just had to rub it in on Tagatz.

Then when Tagatz led the parade of cars past the turn to my place and they all ended up in Crab Orchard, Kentucky, twenty miles from my home, Tim could not let him off without another jab to his pride. This above may give you a better understanding of his poem.

Reunion in Danville

The "twenty-oh-ei ghter" in Danville,
A reunion for the books,
Was fraught with fun and memories,
And even some "mistooks."

Just think of old Tom Lyons,
(The travel agent guy),
Like "Wrongway" Corrigan of old,
He never learned to fly.

Tom meant to go to Lexington;
From there he had a ride,
But he said "I'm in Louis-ville,"
"Where did Lex-ton hide?"

But Ralph came to the rescue,
And really saved the day;
Hosting all of us in Dan-ville,
He was generous that way.

The racehorse club in Keeneland,
Was fun for each and all,
And Tralla really took the cake,
(As Tagatz took a fall.)

But Tagatz made a great comeback,
To lead the trip to Ralph's;
He led us past the right highway,
(He knows his Norths and Souths.)

The joy ride with Doug and Faye,
To "Crab Tree Orchard" town,
Provided added thrills for Tim;
(Doug never lets me down.)
So everything was peachy keen.

TYLER, TEXAS (2009)

This reunion in 2009 was memorable for more than one reason. This reunion turned out to be the twenty-first and last reunion. At the Executive Committee Meeting of the Association, I objected to reimbursing the Lyons for the cost of using an event planner. My objection was that those of us who had volunteered for all the previous reunion had agreed to do the planning, and so had the Lyons. Having hosted three reunions myself, I spent hundreds of unreimbursed monies. So, by vote of the committee, we rejected paying the $1,500 cost. However, I have reason to believe that Tagatz came to the rescue for the Lyons. In any event, it was, next to the event at Max and Marlene Miller's, the best of all the reunions. It was well-planned with a lot of enjoyable activities. A beautiful photo book was sent to everyone after the reunion was over. Since Tom had flown into Louisville instead of Lexington on my last reunion, I told him I was flying into Houston, Texas and gave him a call for pickup. In the end, we are still shipmates and the best of friends.

The Old Bell Crew and Tyler Too

Deep in the heart of Tyler town,
Down Eastern Texas way,
The boys of the "Bell" met one more time,
To rehash yesterday.

Remember the war and shared events,
And what we did back then,
When we were young, and fighting mad,
With World War Two to win.

In Tyler we had quite a show,
Museums by the score,
And dinner on the lake front,
Margaritas by the shore.

Thanks to Tom and Bill and Joy,
Our hosts for this go' round,
The "get together" warmed our hearts,
With ties forever bound.

The laughter, and recounted tales,
May not have all been new,
But every version, new or old,
Still rings as being true.

So hoist a toast to old sea dogs,
And reminisce with me,
While shipmates gather memories,
To cast beyond the sea

CONCLUSION AND FINAL THOUGHTS

I feel proud and honored to be standing among the remaining 497,770 World II veterans who are still alive on August 2, 2019. The Lord willing, I plan to be around a few more years, because I have so many good things going for me. For example, I am in the thirteenth year of a beautiful marriage to my second wife Janice, which is almost as great as my nearly sixty years of marriage to my first wife Charlotte. I am in very good health and am still able to spend an hour in the gym almost daily. I get nothing except first-class care at the Dayton VA, where I get the feeling that I am the only patent who Vickie Burch and her nurse Laura serve.

My goal in life is to tell as many people as possible about those of us who fought in the Pacific Theater of war during WWII. The original book, *Forgotten Warriors,* was the beginning, and this second edition is a continuation of that effort. I welcome the opportunity to speak on the war in the Pacific to groups and organizations. It is not about speaker's fees or book sales; it is about recognition and a lasting memory for all my comrades who fought and died in the vast Pacific Ocean and are now nearly forgotten.

After getting an engineering degree from the University of Kentucky on the GI Bill, I had a fantastic career in electric power engineering, not just in the US, but also all over the world. This is unbelievable for a country boy from central Kentucky who grew up during the Great Depression in very humble surroundings. There is an answer, and you would have to read my first book, *The Power of a Mother's Prayer,* to obtain the information. However, the title should give you a quick clue.

QUESTIONS STILL REMAIN ABOUT THE WAR IN THE PACIFIC

There remain many questions about WWII that are open for debate, including in book club discussions.

1. Was the use of the atomic bomb necessary?
2. Why does the European Theater get all the present-day attention?
3. Was the WWII Museum in New Orleans right in spending the first fifteen years building the road to Berlin before starting the road to Tokyo?
4. Which commander in the Pacific deserves the highest praise (Nimitz, Spruance, Halsey, or MacArthur)?
5. Which battle in the Pacific was the turning point in the war with Japan?
6. What is the likelihood of a WWIII?
7. Which service played the greatest role in defeating Japan?
8. Which was worse for our troops in terms of local conditions: the Aleutian or the Solomon Islands?
9. What did our troops do during WWII to gain recognition as the greatest generation?
10. What has had the greatest effect on the negative attitude of our present-day troops, or is there a negative attitude?

REFERENCES

1. All references for tables came from Scheile US Casual Statistic of American Battles *(www.US/Battle info.ASP)*, Wikipedia, the free encyclopedia *(www.wikipedia.ord)*, or "World War II Death Toll of All Nations" *(www. world/chronical.org)*. (Since discrepancies existed in final numbers, the author used numbers from these sources in the order listed—that is, if numbers were missing from the first source, the second source was used, and so forth.)

   All references for Medal of Honor citations came from US Government Citation; Wikipedia, the free encyclopedia *(www.wikipedia.org)*; the Medal of Honor Society *(www.medalofhonor.org)*; *(http//www.worldwar2history.info/II/Medal-of-Honor/Guam.html)*; or Congressional Medal of Honor Society *(www.themedalofhonor.org)*. Since different sources were used, not all information is consistently stated.

2. References for maps came from *(www.WorldAtlas.)*; University of Kentucky Cardiology Lab (Jacqueline Goins, *www.uky.edu)*; Wikipedia, the free encyclopedia *(www.wikipedia.org)*; GNU Free Documentation License Wikipedia; *(www.historyplace.com.)*

3. References for pictures are cited with each picture— Official US Navy photographs *(http://usnavy photographs/publicdomain.gov)*.

4. All poetry was written by Timothy D. Churchill over the past seventy-five years.
5. *Naval History*, "Peleliu: The Forgotten Battle" by Maj. Henry Donigan (September 1994).
6. *The Power of a Mother's Prayer* by D. Ralph Young Tate, May 2014.
7. *The Girls of Atomic City* by Denise Kiern (2013.
8. "Runway Able" by Ronny Herman de Jong

APPENDIX A: CREW ASSIGNED TO USS J. FRANKLIN BELL: APRIL 2, 1942

Aaron, Hugh (N)

Acord, Donald J.

Adams, John M.

Adams, Silvester (N)

Albersman, Joseph B.

Alexander, Burdatt (N)

Algeo, Edwin H.

Alix, James D.

Allen, Clifford D.

Andrews, Raymond (N)

Agualo, Franciso G.

Arguello, Roman (N)

Arneti, Floyd Y. Jr.

Baglione, Phillip, F.

Bahan, Julius, M.

Bailey, George B.

Baldwin, Joseph 1 C.

Baugus, Melvin E.

Berckhamer, Charles C.

Benson, Raymond E.

Berckhamer, Chlrs.

Berge, Robert G.

Bignell, Ernest H. L.

Blackman, Raymond L.

Blount, Ralph D.

Bluhm, Alfred R.

Boetticher, Oscar G.

Bold, Robert J.

Boynton, William P.

Bradley, O'Dell (N)

Braud, John E. Jr.

Bray, Marvin, John Jr.

Breton, Leonard.

Brett, George T.

Bridge, David D

Brigham, Samuel Jr.

Brinkman, Bernard J.

Brock, William E.

Browne, Robert K.

Bryan, Daniel (N)

Bunn, Kenneth R.

Burns, Ward R.

Burros. Andrew (N)

Campbell, Morgan "JP"

Cannon, Henry W.

Capshaw, Ross L.

Carr, Edward C.

Carter, David (N)

Cartwright, Jessie H.

Ceraso, Frank T.

Chaney, Wesley G.

Choate, William M.

Chan, James (N)

Christian. Dale R.

Ciprian, Michael (N)

Ciscell, Harold L.

Clement, Edward (N)

Clifton, John R.

Cliver, John R.

Clow, Leslie G.

Colley, John C.

Collins, Archiebald

Compton, Earl H.

Corbecky, Domino W.

Conner, James T.

Corboy, Jerome F

Cornwall, Ted J.

Cottrell, George (N)

Cowan, Robert C.

Cox, Joseph (N)

Cranfield, "L" "B"

Crawford, Richard (N)

Creekmore, Bernard T

Curry, Julius G. Jr.

Curtiss, Everett M.

Dahna, Alfred D.

Daill, Garland F.

Danielson, Ronald R.

Davenport, Lloyd W.

Davis, Charles E. Jr.

Davis, Samuel (N)

Davis, William R.

Dean, William E.

Decker, Theo

Defreest, Donald F.

Dehart, Marvin A.

Devlin, William G.

Denson, Augustus M.

Deverra, Genaro (N)

Dewitt, Francis W.

Dewitt, Warren H.

Dewitt, Warren J.

Dietl, Walter J.

Digges, Gilbert (N)

Dinwiddie, James H.

Dinwiddie, Ralph H.

Dungoa, Juan Q.

Durham, Paul A.

Edquist, Herbert E.

Eggleston, Arthur G.

Elkins, Robert E.

Ellis, Francis E.

English, Herbert

Entzminger, Ulysses F.

Ervin, Harrison H.

Evangelista, Eulallo (N)

Evans, Irving (N)

Evans, John E.

Ewing, Sanford L.

Farnsworth, Normand

Decker, Theo (N)

Foster, James A.

Freitas, Henry R.

Frost, Dwight W.

Furman, Donald E.

Gahwiler, Raymond R. Rm

Gallaway, Cecil E.

Galloway, Lawrence H.

Gamble, William F.

Gamblin, Melville A.

Gardner, John E.

Garland, Oscar (N)

Garnett, Nathaniel (N)

Garzione, Thomas (N)

Gear, Robert M.

Gerllca, Joseph F.

Giaimo, John J.

Gillett, Howard L.

Glynn, Robert "J"

Goff, William A.

Gooch, William P.

Goodman, Dan J.

Gordon, Ray M.

Green, John H.

Greenleaf, Fred S.

Griffith, John Joseph

Grindell, Charles E.

Grissom, Firm D.

Groves, Wallace L.

Gunning, John J.

Hacker, Richard L.

Hackler, Lonnie L.

Hajducko, Michael (N)

Hall, Harman W.

Hall, Laird D.

Hall, William J.

Halloran, Thomas R.

Hamilton, Bruce F.

Hamilton, Jack G.

Hammock, James C.

Hancock, John H.

Hankins, Charles L.

Hansen, Carl (N)

Hardacre, Richard E.

Harrigan, Martin D.

Harris, George B.

Harrison, William A.

Hart, Robert W.

Hartman, Harvey "A"

Hawker, Everett J.

Hawkins, Bill (N)

Hay, Colbert T.

Headlly, Milton F.

Henry, William H.

Herbert, Anthony M.

Herriman, Richard F.

Hess, Gerald H.

Hills, Burch M.

Hinkle, Thomas F.

Hinners, Norman E.

Hiter, Charles (N)

Hodge, James E.

Hoehn, Donald J.

Hoffman, Frederick (N)

Hoffman, Robert D.	Lohrman, Joseph D.
Holmes, Julius A.	Lomat, Venancio (N)
Holshouser, Jesse A.	Lowitz, Carl A.
Honsinger, Emerson G.	Lupton, Vincent D.
Hood, Delbert B.	Mabayak, Jose (N)
Hooten, Roland W.	Maki, Chester L.
Hoover, Harold V.	Manderson, James T.
Hopkins, Wallace R.	Marino, Ralph T.
Houch, John D.	Martin, James H. Jr.
Hovland, Luther J.	Martin, Max E.
Hudak, Steve (N)	Martin, Walter
Hudson, John R.	Matson, Keith C.
Hughes, William E.	Mathews, William P. Jr.
Hughey, Eugene Leroy	Mattson, Harold H.
Hunnicutt, Robert B.	May, Louis (N)
Hutton, Richard L.	McBride, Donald F.
Ivie, Edward V.	McCabe, James P.
Jackson, Claude L.	McCahen, Walter D.
Lay, Robert L.	McCorkle, James W.
Leath, James C.	McDonald, William P.
Lee, James G.	McIlrath, Jesse D.
Lenard, Herbert C.	McKellop. James A.
Lenarski, Stanley J.	McKinney, Frank B.
Lesh, Clyde R.	McMaster, Mack E.
Lester, Ian V.	McNamee, Earl M.
Lewis, Howard N.	McNatt, Robert H.
Leyde, Carl B.	McQuarrie, Alfred A.
Liles, Barnnie R.	McShea, Bernard (N)
Llnday, John H.	Mead, Jack W.
Lineberry, Loren L.	Messinger, Elmer E.

Meyer, Clifford R.

Miles, Aubrey A.

Miller, Carroll S.

Miller, Charles C.

Miller, Clyde W.

Miller, John Jr. (N)

Milner, Aubray A.

Miller, Douglas R.

Mitchell, William V.

Mize, Robert C.

Mooney, James J.

Moore, Albert F.

Moore, Loen C.

Moore, Milton M.

Morano, Patsy (N)

Murel, Nicholas (N)

Myers, Howard E.

Myers, Ray (N)

Nash, Robert H.

Nava, Juan L.

Nerim, Alvin A.

Nesany, Bruce B.

Neville, John J.

Obelles, Robert R.

O'Brien, Jack R.

O'Connor, James E.

Odaware, Phillip L.

Olcott, Byron R.

Oldack, Edwin (N)

Oliver, Robert J.

Oppenheimer, Benjamin

Osborne, Francis M.

Ott, William C.

Owen, Gerald R.

Paarman, Eugene M.

Palker, James L.

Palmer, Harold R.

Palmer, Sharwood H.

Parsons, Quentin (N)

Patrick, Earl S.

Patten, Myrne R.

Paxton, Freeman E.

Peacock, Darrel Y.

Pearman, Max "B"

Peck, William E.

Peloquin, Ferdinand C.

Peters, Rodger E.

Peterson, Leroy (N)

Philbrick, Russell A.

Phillips, Patrick (N)

Pierce, Joseph C.

Pilkington, Albert X.

Pokatello, John (N)

Poland, Jack (N)

Pollitt, Robert E.

Pomeroy, Daniel E.

Powell, Theodore S.

Priest, Bill E.

Pulaski, Elmer R.

Pulis, Lorin H.

Ramborger, William O.

Ramey, James H.

Ramsey, Collier

Rawn, Robert D.

Reading, Thomas A.

Reed, Ernest D.

Reed, Thomas H.

Reichlin, Joseph J.

Renner, Clarance H.

Reno, Robert J.

Reyes, Aroenic (N)

Richardson, Frank E.

Richmand+

+-, Roy F.

Riley, William J.

Roberts, Curry A. Jr.

Roberts, Leo A.

Robinson, Darvin E.

Rodgers, Alphonso (N)

Roley, William R.

Rolfe, Donald R.

Romaniak, Frank

Romero, Robert "E"

Rose, Victor (N)

Rowe, Phil M.

Ryan, Francis P.

Sablan, Antonio L.

Sablin, Juan T.

Salatka, Edward A.

Sal Ter, George W.

Sanford, Billie P.

Sargent, Harvey E.

Sauer, Carl J.

Saunders, Charlie

Sayles, Edward P.

Scaley, Harold A.

Schadee, Richard W.

Schaffneer, Robert J.

Schenk, Edgar O.

Scherber, Eugene E.

Schrader, Donnell E.

Scott, George A. Jr.

Scott. Lloyd E.

Scott, Wilbur (N)

Searles, Roy W.

Sehrier, Joseph M.

Selak, Frank (N)

Severson, Russell M.

Shank, Charles R.

Sheets, Michael L.

Shepard, William M.

Silakowski, Michael J.

Silvers, Harold C.

Simas, Williams (N)

Simmons, Roy D.

Skeley, Harold A.

Slater, Harry S.

Slaughter, Roy A. Jr.

Slayton, Zachary T.

Smith, Charles J.

Smith, Earl C. Jr.

Souza, John S.

Spalding, Louis R.

Spivey, Roy L.

Squires, Robert P.

Stabenow, Glenn C.

Stanchfield, William B.

Stanfield, James E.

Stanley, John B.

Stapleton, James A.

Staron, Frank W.

Starr, Willard D.

Steinhoff, Wilbur C.

Stephenson, Thomas M.

Stettler, Carl E.

Stimmler, Hugo M.

Stock, Francis A.

Stoneburner, John R.

Stoner, Harley J.

Stophel, Robert E.

Strait, Russell W.

Strawn, Warren A.

Strickland, Roy A.

Stutzman, Warren L.

Swaney, Marlo (N)

Tagatz, Robert C.

Taylor, William E.

Thomas, George A.

Thompson, "J" D.

Thompson, Dallas L.

Thompson, Richard K.

Thourman, Eddie (N)

Tipton, Harold N.

Tirlot, Eugene D.

Todd, Paul A.

Tourtelotte, Chester L.

Townsend, Carl Alvin

Tralla, Wade A.

Trice, James (N)

Turner, Ottis (N)

Van Court, Louis T.

Van Decar, James W.

Van Wager, Robert (N)

Vaughn, James H.

Vincent, Howard R.

Visich, John (N)

Wade, James P.

Wahlborg, Clyde G.

Wanbaugh, Calvin C.

Warnock, George G.

Washington, Charles L.

Watkins, William G.

Weaver, James R.

Weber, Fred (N)

Wells, Harold E.

Wells, Lawrence A.

Wentzel, Glenn I.

Werth, Kenneth L.

West, Archie A.

Wilson, Robert W.

Winters, William F.
Wise, Franklin N.
Wood, Jack B.
Wood, Jack J.
Woods, Morris W.
Worshek, Harry L.
Wylie, Donald L.

APPENDIX B: MEDAL OF HONOR RECIPIENTS IN WWII

Printed in the United States
By Bookmasters